LET GO, LET MIRACLES HAPPEN

Let Go, Let Miracles Happen

THE ART OF SPIRITUAL SURRENDER

Kathy Cordova

CONARI PRESS

First published in 2003 by Conari Press,
an imprint of Red Wheel/Weiser, LLC
York Beach, ME
With offices at:
368 Congress Street
Boston, MA 02210
www.redwheelweiser.com

Library of Congress Cataloging-in-Publication Data

Cordova, Kathy.
   Let go, let miracles happen : the art of spiritual surrender /
Kathy Cordova.
       p. cm.
Includes bibliographical references (p. 198).
   ISBN 1-57324-874-6
   1. Spiritual life. 2. Submissiveness—Religious aspects. 3. Self-
actualization (Psychology)—Religious aspects. I. Title.
   BL624.C6653 2003
   204'.4—dc22   2003013995

Typeset in Dante and Scala Sans
Designed and typeset by Gopa & Ted2, Inc.
Printed in Canada
Printed by TCP

10 09 08 07 06 05 04 03
 8 7 6 5 4 3 2 1

To Savannah and Carson,
who are teaching me the joy of surrender.

contents

acknowledgments

$\mathcal{M}$Y HEARTFELT THANKS to everyone who played a part in the creation of this book:

To my husband, Jeff, for your unwavering support and belief in me. Thanks also for my fabulous website, for Sundays to write, and for my lucky spoontop. I love you.

To M.J. Ryan, for your insight, faith, and generosity of spirit. This book could never have been written without your guidance.

Bunches of hugs and a big glass of cabernet to the Divine LLs—Amy Moellering, Cameron Sullivan, Grace Navalta, and Keely Parrack. Thank you for your exquisite editorial feedback with the perfect blend of brutal honesty, genuine affection, and enthusiastic cheerleading. Your friendship means more than I can say.

To my mother and father, Tenny Jo and Ronald Hill, for always being there with love and acceptance. You have given me the roots that have allowed me to fly. You are my models of what is truly good in this world, and I love you with all my heart.

To the amazing folks at Conari Press: Jan Johnson, Jill Rogers, Lucine Kasbarian, Brenda Knight, Pam Suwinsky, Robyn Heisey, Emily Sauber, Liz Wood, Kathleen Fivel and Kate Hartke, for all your hard work and devotion to this project. Thanks for giving me the perfect place for birthing this book.

To everyone who has been a positive force in my life during the unfolding of this book: Ame Beanland, Jeb Bing, Betty Branham, Dolores Ciardelli, Amy Gephart, Dawn Gordner, Christina Nunes, Jim Ott, Denise Roy, Kelly Boyer Sagert, Darla Stevens, Barbara Tavres, and Sheila Tole. Thank you for opportunities given, wisdom bestowed, or encouraging words spoken.

And most importantly, my thanks to all the contributors for so generously transforming the lessons of your heartaches and your joys into the words of this book. You are an inspiration, and I am blessed to share your stories.

introduction

TOLERANCE FOR PAIN MAY BE HIGH, BUT IT IS NOT
WITHOUT LIMIT. EVENTUALLY EVERYONE BEGINS
TO RECOGNIZE, HOWEVER DIMLY, THAT THERE MUST
BE A BETTER WAY.
— *A COURSE IN MIRACLES*

I HAD AN INKLING there was a better way a long time ago, but it took a lot of wrong turns to find it.

I have to confess: I am one of the world's biggest self-help junkies. Like a lot of people, I've been intoxicated with the idea that I'm in control, and I've been seduced into believing that I'm just one good book or workshop away from my ideal self. Like any true addict, there was never enough of what I needed and I was never enough regardless of what I achieved.

Most of us grew up with the message that we're not enough—not thin enough, not smart enough, not pretty enough, not "in love" enough. Look at the movies we watch and the magazines we read: we are utterly inadequate when compared to our media-inspired fantasies. We look for our fixes everywhere—in psychotherapy, Prozac, Botox, Prince or Princess Charming, or self-help books that promise magic.

We're always hoping that right around the corner is the magic formula that will erase the wrinkles, get rid of that extra 10 pounds, reveal our true love, and make us happy.

The bad news is, there is no magic formula. The fixes are temporary at best. The wrinkles come back, and so do the 10 pounds. Our true love is never quite everything we imagined he or she would be. Happiness is elusive, transitory, or seemingly impossible in a world of escalating expectations.

The good news is, there's an alternative to the struggle to fix ourselves magically—another way that will lead us to peace and prosperity beyond our limited mind's ability to contemplate. The good news is miracles. Instead of working so hard to find or create magic in our lives, we can relax, go with the flow, work together in harmony with a power greater than ourselves, and experience more love, joy, and purpose than we ever imagined. And the formula is simple: love and surrender.

Or, at least it sounds simple, according to many of the spiritual books out there. But love and surrender are not what the world teaches us. We are taught to struggle and compete, to look out for number 1, and to get an eye for an eye. Even if we're not Machiavellian, we are convinced that we need to control every aspect of our lives in order to achieve true happiness. Being out of control terrifies us, and surrender often seems like a last resort for losers.

We may be able to love and surrender when everything's going okay. It's easy to love people who are nice to you and to go with the flow when life is working. But how do you love the spouse who cheats on you? Or the boss who takes credit for your work? Or the neighbor who talks about you behind your back? And how do you go with the flow when it seems like the world is crashing all around you?

There must be a better way, but the path is not clear. We look to spiritual books for guidance and comfort. They sound wonderful with their big ideas, wise words, and soothing prayers. We read them and we are inspired. We *believe* them, but when it comes to *practicing* their lessons, we are left wondering if, like high school calculus, they're actually something we can use in the real world.

Self-help books, on the other hand, are practical. They are full of numbered lessons and exercises, punchy anecdotes, and uplifting affirmations. But they often appeal to our rational minds and leave our spirits thirsting for more. These books tell us how to find the perfect job, perfect lover, or perfect body, but there's a piece missing. This piece that is missing prevents us from achieving these fabulous things in our lives, or if we do meet our goals, leaves us inexplicably unsatisfied. We're like junkies who need increasingly bigger fixes to give us the same level of pleasure. So we keep running to the next deal, job, relationship, or diet book, looking for more.

Take it from me; I've read all those books. I have dozens of volumes on my shelves about following my bliss, thinking and growing rich, or awakening my giant within. I've also read my share of spiritual books. I'm a sucker for any sharp-talking author on *Oprah* or a book jacket that promises enlightenment in thirty days.

The combination of the two genres—self-help and spiritual—buzzing around in my brain left me more confused than ever about how to live. Do I *go for it* or *go with the flow*? Do I set goals and visualize or do I surrender my will to the wisdom of a Higher Power? Do I analyze and think? Or do I pray and follow my intuition?

I've spent nearly twenty years testing and synthesizing these diverse messages. In that time, I believe I've discovered the missing piece of the puzzle that makes everything fit together. This piece leads us to a much more magnificent life than we could ever dream, while still living in alignment with our inner knowledge and a universal Higher Power of goodness and love.

The missing piece is *spiritual surrender*. Not a "loser" kind of surrender. Spiritual surrender is an awakening and an awareness that our rational mind and our ego are not the highest powers in the Universe. Spiritual surrender is letting go of the struggles in our lives and tapping into something that is much greater than ourselves yet is found within ourselves when we make the connection with a universal Higher Power.

Even though we've all heard advice to "surrender" and "let it go" and "go with the flow," nobody ever tells us *what* to surrender, or *how* to let it go, or *how to find* the flow that we're supposed to be going with.

I've discovered that *surrender* is a broad term that encompasses four different types of issues, each with its own universal principles:

1. *Letting go* of what is not working in our lives, whether it's painful feelings, limiting beliefs, or specific situations. Some examples of things we may need to release are anger, need for approval, ego, fear, or a miserable job or failed relationship. By letting go of destructive feelings,

behaviors, and situations or unrealistic expectations we can learn to accept what is true in our lives and move forward.

 The principle: Whatever you are holding onto most tightly is probably the exact thing you need to let go of. Whatever you're most afraid of losing may be what you need to release to make way for something better.

2. *Surrendering a problem* is simply giving our troubles to God/a Higher Power/the Universe. This is often a surrender of last resort, although it doesn't need to be.

 The principle: You can surrender any problem—large or small—to God and know you will get the perfect answer. Then it is up to you to accept and act on that answer.

3. *Going with the flow* means giving up our belief in struggle and learning to swim with the current in our lives and the Divine guidance of our intuition.

 The principle: Stop fighting. Stop struggling. Go with your intuition. Avoid the things that don't feel *right*, despite what your logical mind tells you. Once you release your fears and connect with your flow, life will unfold perfectly.

4. *Surrendering to love* means letting go of the barriers to love in our lives. It means perceiving only love and giving only love back.

 The principle: See the love inherent in every person and situation. Sometimes it seems there is only hopelessness, sadness, grief, or tragedy. Seek out the love and then act only with love. When you give love and peace, you will receive love and peace in your life.

✍ How to Read This Book

This book is structured a little differently than most books:
The first part of this book—chapters 1 and 2—explores my

experiences and philosophies about spiritual surrender. These are revelations gained not from gurus on Himalayan mountaintops but in the context of lousy bosses, disappointing relationships, and tantrum-throwing toddlers. I consider myself a "spiritual journalist"—an investigative reporter of Divine guidance and destiny using my own experiences for material. These chapters chronicle my path to spiritual surrender, which has happened for me—the most rational and goal-oriented of people—in slow, start-and-stop bursts—lots of baby steps. At first I let go only a little. When I didn't fall (or I fell, but got right back up), I learned to trust and let go a little more. It was a steady practice of surrender, until I felt not only safe but exhilaratingly free, like a baby who has just discovered the joy of walking.

These chapters are meant to be simple and practical—lessons and principles that you will be able to relate to and put into practice in your own life. I hoped to create something that would be valuable to readers at any points on their spiritual paths—as a foundation if your journey is just beginning, or as reinforcement, grounded in real-life examples, if you are far along on your path.

Because I believe stories are our most powerful and enduring teachers, the second part of the book—Chapters 3 through 6—is comprised of the tales of ordinary people who have forgiven their parents, quit miserable (yet secure) jobs, given up alcohol or drugs, decided to follow their hearts and intuition to their destiny, or surrendered themselves to love during the grief of caring for a dying child.

These stories are some of the most intimate, miraculous, and inspiring stories I have ever read. As you read about these remarkable, generous souls and share their most painful experiences, their most heart-rending vulnerabilities, and their ultimate joys, I believe you will find yourself transformed, as I have been.

My wish is that you come away from this book with the inspiration and the knowledge to experience the power of spiritual surrender in your life. May you be open to receiving all the peace and happiness that is your own Divine destiny.

CHAPTER 1

miracles, not magic:
MY PATH TO SPIRITUAL SURRENDER

MAGIC IS THE MINDLESS OR MISCREATIVE USE OF THE MIND.

CONSCIOUSLY SELECTED MIRACLES CAN BE MISGUIDED.

MIRACLES OCCUR NATURALLY AS EXPRESSIONS OF LOVE.
THE REAL MIRACLE IS THE LOVE THAT INSPIRES THEM. IN THIS
SENSE EVERYTHING THAT COMES FROM LOVE IS A MIRACLE.

—*A COURSE IN MIRACLES*

I've always been very good at *making* things happen.
I visualized and affirmed my way from blue-collar roots
to a six-figure income, a red BMW convertible, and a private office
with a view of the San Francisco Bay. Coming of age in the '80s, I
truly believed that if I wanted something badly enough, I could *make*
it happen.

What I wanted most to happen were money and success—two
things that were pretty elusive when I was a kid. My mother and
father were completely devoted to their children; we felt safe and
loved, and I know I was luckier than a lot of kids. But it was hard
watching my father struggle, working two jobs to barely pay the
bills, while my mother stayed home, taking care of my three brothers and me. I vaguely remember Dad talking about opening his own
sporting goods store "someday," and Mom saying she always wanted
to be a lawyer, but these were just pipe dreams—nothing they ever
really believed would happen.

My parents were the kind of regular working people who didn't
make things happen—things happened *to* them. Their ambitions

were all the obligatory goals of a young family working hard to make ends meet—stretching the milk and bread to last until the next payday or paying the minimum balance on their Sears card every month.

I was determined to be different. I studied hard and was the first in my family to go to college. I put myself through school with a combination of sheer force of will, scholarships, and waiting a lot of tables.

After I graduated, I got a job in computer sales purely because of the potential to make lots of money, and that was my focus. When I saw Tony Robbins—the motivational guru—on a late-night infomercial, I was mesmerized. I had found the answer to my struggles. Robbins preached *Awaken the Giant Within,* and that's exactly what I did. I bought his *Personal Power* tapes for $369.99 and listened to them every day on my Walkman while I climbed the Stairmaster. The trainer at my health club used to joke that I was just a little orgy of self-improvement.

Listening to the motivational tapes, setting goals, and religiously doing affirmations for what I wanted to materialize in my life worked like magic. Out of thin air, I created my own reality, exactly as advertised.

Soon I was flying 100,000 first-class miles a year, negotiating million-dollar contracts across mahogany boardroom tables, and winning trips to the Caribbean for exceeding my quotas.

I was in complete control of my life, and I left nothing to chance. I consistently *willed* myself to win deals that should have been beyond my reach. Once I was trying to win a new account, and I knew the director of computer services was already sold on my competitor's product, which was based on big-name, cutting-edge technology. Our product, in contrast, was older and more reliable, but not exciting enough for the young, ambitious director who was leading the selection process. Things didn't look good for me, so on the day of the committee meeting to decide the winning company, I played subliminal prosperity tapes under the desk in my office while I persuaded and cajoled each committee member on the phone before the meeting. The magic worked again. At the end of the day, I got the news that the sale was mine.

Soon all my dreams were coming true. Not only was I a top per-
former at work, I was happily married and pregnant with my first
child. I had achieved every goal I'd ever wanted but, strangely, I didn't
feel content. I was making plenty of money, but the job was overwhelming, stressful—a constant struggle. I felt like there was something else out there I was supposed to be doing, although I didn't
know what. But I wouldn't allow myself to dwell on these issues.
Whenever I had twinges about something missing, I chased them
away with the adrenaline of closing another deal and cashing a big
commission check.

Having a baby raised even more doubts about what I *should* be
doing. I wondered if I should quit my job and stay home with my
child the way my mother had with us, but I was terrified at the
thought of giving up my income and being poor again. I was making
twice as much money as my self-employed husband, and leaving my
job felt very financially risky. I couldn't bring myself to take that
chance. The money and the status of my career were too seduc-
tive—I wasn't ready to give them up. So the plan was to take a four-
month maternity leave, then hire a nanny and go back to work.

Only things didn't go as planned.

My baby daughter was colicky—or, as our pediatrician put it more
accurately, *very colicky*. She cried all day, every day. Instead of the
blissful maternity leave of long naps and trips to the park I had envisioned, those first months were pure misery for both of us. She cried
and I cried, every single day. I couldn't wait to go back to work.

But finding a nanny was harder than we thought. We must have
tried out twenty different caregivers. My daughter would scream
relentlessly at each and every one of them for hours on end. Most of
them never came back after the first day and wouldn't even return my
phone calls.

We hobbled along for a month, with me mostly working at home
and sharing childcare duties with my husband and the parade of
"trial" nannies that swept through our house. I was torn between
my responsibilities at work and my responsibilities at home, between
the huge rewards of my job and the instinctual tugging at my heart
that told me I needed to be home with my daughter.

Finally, the day before my first postpartum business trip, I did the least rational and most intuitive thing of my life—I quit my job.

My boss offered to reschedule the trip. He offered to go on the trip in my place, in order to give me more time to get settled at home. He did everything he could to change my mind, but I had made my decision. Everyone at work thought I was nuts. Not only was I leaving a great job and territory that I'd worked years to build, but I was also leaving behind a small fortune in commissions that were collectible only if I remained employed.

Leaving all that money on the table was one of the hardest things I've ever done. It was enough money to send my daughter to any university she desired for four years, and then some. For a girl who waited tables to put herself through college, it was a leap of faith to give up this kind of future security for my daughter.

But I knew she needed me then, and we'd just have to let the future take care of itself. For the first time in my life, I surrendered my goals, my preconceived plans, and the logic of my head, to follow the path of my heart.

My mother was especially amused. She found it ironic that I'd been able to accomplish all these great things out in the world, but it took a little baby to bring me to my knees. She was right. If you want a crash lesson in surrender, have a baby—better yet, have a colicky baby.

The Quakers have a saying, "Way closes, way opens," meaning that when one path has ended, another one will open up for us. I didn't learn those words until years later but they were certainly true for me. Once I closed the way to the job and the money that I'd struggled so hard to achieve, other, more gratifying ways of life opened.

It has not always been easy, but the time spent with my daughter—and now her brother—opened my heart in ways I could never have imagined.

But beyond the delights of motherhood, old dreams opened up, too. A local community center class rekindled my passion for writing, long ago buried under the rubble of my success. Within a year of taking that first class, I had been published, appeared on *Oprah,* and began to work as a freelance writer and local cable talk show host. The gush of opportunity that flowed to me was truly beyond my wildest dreams, and, amazingly, was able to fit around my family in a way I never would have believed it could.

My old successes had been struggles, requiring strict control of my mind to make "magic" of my own creation. In contrast, my new successes seemed to be orchestrated by a power who knew me better than I knew myself—and who was a lot kinder to me, too. Opportunities flowed perfectly into one another, almost effortlessly, as if I had finally caught my big wave and was riding it joyously to shore. By surrendering my will and the logic of my rational mind, I experienced a power much more potent than magic. I experienced miracles.

Of course, surrendering my will didn't mean I just lay on the couch, eating chocolate, and asking the Universe to serve me. I worked hard moving toward my dreams—taking classes, jumping at every opportunity, and giving my all to every project, no matter how small. But the work was joyful, not drudgery, and it always felt "right."

I knew everything had changed for me when I called my mother to tell her they were paying me to host a local talk show. She squealed to my father in the next room, "Kathy's getting *paid* to be on TV, and it isn't hard work and she *likes* it!"

I never would have thought so at the time, but I now believe my daughter's colic was destiny. Maybe I needed all that screaming to drown out all my own "should be" self-talk and allow me to listen to my true inner voice.

I'm still pretty good at making things happen. But now I'm a lot better at *letting* things happen—going through the open doors and not trying to push through those that are slammed shut. And I now know that what lies behind those unexpected openings is often much better than I could have ever made happen on my own.

I hope that by sharing my experiences in this pages and the experiences of others, I can show how you, too, can discover the power of spiritual surrender and realize the miracles it can create in your life.

what is spiritual surrender?

THE SUPREME ART OF WAR IS TO SUBDUE THE ENEMY
WITHOUT FIGHTING. —SUN TZU, *THE ART OF WAR*

WHEN I WAS SELLING SOFTWARE, the president of my company insisted that all the salespeople read *The Art of War*, a classic book of military strategy written more than 2,000 years ago by a brilliant Chinese general. We were commanded to read this book and consider ourselves "at war" with our competition, utilizing the strategies of the cunning general to achieve victory on the battlefields of our future customers.

The competitive nature of my job was a given—I knew sales was all about winning. Even so, I was at a point in my life where declaring "war" seemed profoundly at odds with my own burgeoning spirituality. As I read, prayed, and grew spiritually, I realized my goal was peace, not war.

I also realized that while my president was perhaps extreme in his approach, most of us are at war every day, in many aspects of our lives, without even realizing it. In rivalries with coworkers to get the coveted promotion, in competition with other parents to get our kids into the best schools, in battles with our loved ones over money, sex, or dirty socks on the floor.

Most ironic of all, we're constantly at war with ourselves to stick to our diets, get a better job, make more money, be the perfect parent, and beating ourselves up when we lose our personal battles. We were raised to believe in the American dream of struggling and achieving. Our mantras have been "Keep your nose to the grindstone," and "No pain, no gain."

But the pain wasn't always worth the gain and making it happen hasn't necessarily made us happy.

Some of us put our noses to the wrong grindstone. Some of us ground our noses to shreds and missed our kids' childhoods, or missed having children altogether, and then got laid off in the economic downturn anyway. Despite our best efforts, we may have experienced failure and disappointment, leaving us doubting our own power as well as the benevolence of the Universe.

Or maybe we succeeded. Maybe we barged ahead and got the job, the house, or the romantic partner we always thought we wanted, then discovered we still weren't happy. The sculpted biceps and big houses didn't really fill that empty place in our souls that we thought they would. The moment we reached one rung on the ladder of success, we immediately had our eye on the next step—certain it would be the solution to our discontent. Maybe we looked for answers in sex or Chardonnay or money, or even more work, but none of those things filled us either.

So what now? We continue to look for the magic bullet that will end our struggles, point us in the right direction, and make us feel purposeful and at peace. We know there's got to be an answer out there somewhere if we could just figure it out.

There *is* a solution to our disappointments, our anxieties, and our struggles, but it's traditionally the last resort for warriors yearning for peace.

The solution we crave is surrender.

Discovering the Art of Spiritual Surrender

TAKE YOUR HANDS OFF THE STEERING WHEEL. BE ABLE TO SAY TO
THE UNIVERSE, "THY WILL BE DONE," . . . AND ALLOW YOUR LIFE
TO GO INTO THE HANDS OF THE UNIVERSE COMPLETELY.
—GARY ZUKOV, *THE SEAT OF THE SOUL*

From the moment I heard about the concept of spiritual surrender, I was fascinated. I was in my twenties, and some of my friends were pursuing *A Course in Miracles,* a spiritual self-study program. When

I was growing up, I had gone to church every Sunday. I believed in God and considered myself a Christian. But as an adult, I wasn't actively practicing any form of spirituality other than praying for the next sale to close or the next guy to call, and then only after my own best efforts were failing. My friends all raved about the lessons of the Course, and I began to notice myself drawn to people who were studying it. I was intrigued enough to go out a buy a copy of the book for myself.

When I first heard the title *A Course in Miracles*, I thought, "Great! More magic to help me achieve!" I'd already mastered volumes of motivational courses. Now it was time to take things up a notch and experience some miracles!

Reading the text, I was surprised not to find more motivational magic. This book wouldn't show me how to win a sale or think my way to success. Instead, I discovered a course of study, based in the language of Christianity, that proclaims our universal oneness, teaches us to live in love instead of fear, and advises us to surrender to God rather than pursuing the path of our own misguided egos.

The words soothed me. Just reading the Course relieved my anxieties and made me feel more loving. It intuitively felt right. The words spoke to my heart in a way that made sense to my head, too.

I liked the idea that we are all one, like drops of water in the ocean. Since I had spent my whole life being fearful of everything from spiders to commitment, the promise that I could replace my fear with love gave me hope. Practicing these concepts was challenging, I thought, but doable.

The tough piece of the spiritual puzzle for me, however, was surrendering my will and my ego. Even though I instinctively felt that "surrender" was right, I bristled at the idea. Actually, it terrified me. I was so used to controlling every aspect of my life that I couldn't imagine releasing any element of it to a Higher Power who might be busy with more important things. Better for me to be in charge. Surely I knew more about managing my life and getting what I wanted than anybody else—even God. Or so I thought.

Like most people, I'd never been given any guidance about surrender while I was growing up. On the surface, my family *looked* surrendered—they had no true goals, and they did seem to go with the flow. But they really were more beaten down by life than consciously surrendering to it—they were drifting rather than flowing. And that was not what I wanted!

Also, since there was never any extra money to go around, I knew that if I wanted something, it was up to me—and me alone—to get it. When, at the age of sixteen, I decided I needed my teeth fixed, I found the orthodontist, scheduled the appointments close enough together so I'd get the braces off the week before I left for college, and made monthly payments from the money I made at my after-school job. I knew I wanted to go to college, so I researched schools and financial aid, and paid for tuition, room, board, and books. I believed there wasn't a problem I couldn't solve myself with determination, planning, and hard work. I learned to become fiercely independent, ultra "in control," and goal-oriented.

By the time I reached my twenties my goals were to make as much money as possible, buy a house, and travel to Europe. Spiritual surrender would have to wait. Once I got everything I wanted, then maybe I could start surrendering.

In my job, getting the sale was hammered into my head constantly. I once had a sales manager, Tony, who liked to call me from Chicago at 6 A.M. California time and make me take the phone into the bathroom, look into the mirror, and repeat out loud, "I want the order *now!*" And I was getting the orders. I was making my sales and achieving my desired results. I was winning professionally and financially, so there was no outwardly compelling reason to surrender.

Early in my career, I did some interview role-plays with a recruiter who was coaching me. In the middle of the standard interview questions, he threw me a curve. "If you weren't a salesperson, what would you want to be?" he asked. I was stumped. I had no idea what the "right" answer was. He shook his head and said, "An actress, of course."

It took years for the relevance of that remark to sink in, but eventually I understood. No matter how great the rewards, and how much I tried to control my life, I still felt like I was acting a part in a script that somebody else had written. I was tired of acting—I wanted to write my own script, but I was afraid of bad reviews. I had a hunch that surrender would lead me to a more authentic life, but I had no idea what surrender really meant or how to practice it.

Winning Through Surrender

For most of us, the word *surrender* has a negative connotation. We think surrendering means waving the white flag and giving up. We're taught from childhood that quitters never win and winners never quit. Surrender is the last thing we want to do.

Our dictionaries give the word the same negative spin. Webster defines *surrender* as "To give (oneself) up to the power of another especially as a prisoner."

A further definition begins more positively, even passionately: "Abandon or devote (as oneself) entirely to something without restraint, reservation or further resistance." But it quickly adds the cautionary example, "The individual has surrendered himself to destructive ideologies."

The notion of spiritual surrender is quite different.

Spiritual surrender is *not* about defeat; it is about acceptance, joy, and faith. Surrender is about ending the struggle in our lives and beginning our journey on a path more wonderful than we could imagine. As Marianne Williamson says in her book, *A Return to Love,* "Surrender means the decision to stop fighting the world, and to start loving it instead. It is a gentle liberation from pain. . . . To relax, to feel the love in your heart and keep to that as your focus in every situation—that's the meaning of spiritual surrender."

Spiritual surrender is admitting that we're not in control. It's getting ourselves out of the way and trusting a Higher Power to guide us. Spiritual surrender frees us from fear and anger, gives us answers to difficult dilemmas, points us in the right direction, and grants us peace. Spiritual surrender can lead us to a life that is more joyful and abundant than we ever dreamed.

Another great misconception about surrender is that it's an escape for the lazy. But spiritual surrender isn't about doing nothing, waiting for God to hand you a wonderful new life on a silver platter.

Quite the contrary, surrender can actually spur you to action, but it will be joyous, loving action rather than manipulative striving. Buddhists call it "compassionate action."

As Buddhist nun Pema Chödrön says in her book, *Start Where You Are: A Guide to Compassionate Living,* "Compassionate action is the importance of working *with* rather than struggling *against*. It's keeping your heart and your mind open to whatever arises, without hope of fruition."

Chödrön also tells us, "Abandon any hope of fruition. You could also say, 'Give up all hope' or 'Give up' or just 'Give.' The shorter the better."

To give freely—without selfish motives—is one of the quickest and surest routes to spiritual surrender. When I was selling software, though, such an idea was still foreign to me. I remember one particularly frustrating dilemma.

Our company sold computer systems to colleges and universities, notorious for big committees, convoluted politics, and long, long sales cycles. But one small school I was working with was breaking all records. We'd spent years doing demonstrations, answering hundreds of questions, squiring them to corporate headquarters and client sites, and still they could not make up their minds.

At the end of the quarter, my boss pressured me to do whatever it took to close the sale. By this time, I was tired of working on this deal, and I thought I had tried everything. I was tired of all the personalities at this college, and I cringed whenever I got yet another request for more information. I was about to throw in the towel, but I'd already invested so much time and energy that I hated the idea of just giving up. So I didn't give up. Instead, I gave the situation to God.

So I prayed, "Dear God, please help me to be more understanding, more compassionate. Help me to guide these people to the correct decision, whatever that may be." Words of love and peace—not war and conflict.

I instantly felt release of all the stress I'd had about the situation. It was like a bolt of lightning struck my self-serving attitude, melting away my hostility and recharging my reserves of compassion. Suddenly, I felt warmth and love—instead of exasperation—toward my customers! I was now seeing things from their point of view;

this was a decision that would cost them hundreds of thousands of dollars. I could make the sale and move on to the next deal, but they would have to live with their decision for years, and the success of their organization depended on it.

Now it was clear to me that it was my job to help them get all the information necessary to make them feel comfortable with their decision. I recommitted myself to diligently answering every single question, not in a manipulative or angry, resentful way, but in a truly loving, concerned manner. I decided my job was not to *get the sale*, but just to *love* my customer.

That was a turning point. There was a huge, discernible shift in our relationship. I'm sure they could feel the difference in my attitude toward them—love replacing my fear and impatience—*working with* instead of *struggling against* them.

Soon afterward, they decided to purchase our system, and the college became one of my most loyal customers and a wonderful reference.

This was also one of my first experiences of true surrender. Clearly, it was not an example of defeat, and it wasn't the lazy way out. Instead, it was a relaxed, caring, joyful way of doing business that turned out great for everyone; the customer got the information and support necessary to make a good decision, and I got the sale.

This is a great example of how surrender is an "inside job." I didn't have to surrender the sale to do the right thing. The only thing I had to let go of was the way I *thought* about the sale. Most of the things we need to surrender are creations of our own minds—our own perceptions that make our life hell.

I didn't win every deal by operating out of love, but I won a lot. And whenever I worked at loving my customer instead of merely selling her, I always felt at peace with myself and the situation—win or lose.

Yet there have been many times when I have resisted surrender.

✍ What We Resist Persists

One of the best reasons for surrendering is that what we resist persists. Anyone who's parented a toddler knows how true this is; "No" is their favorite word. A two-year-old will resist anything and everything; my kids have even resisted ice cream when they're in particularly negative moods! The more we engage them in a struggle, the longer the resistance lasts. The more we push, the harder they push back.

The idea that what we resist persists is as true for emotions as it is for toddler behavior. How many times have we *tried not to be* angry, or hurt, or fearful, only to feel these emotions amplified? Often, we'll try to deny or stuff the feelings, only to find them percolating until they explode like an ancient volcano that's been churning below the surface for years.

When I first quit my job after having a baby, one of the biggest ongoing battles I had with my husband was about lunch. He worked out of an office in our house, and every day he liked to have the same exact thing for lunch—a ham and cheese sandwich, on a certain kind of bread, with a certain kind of chips and his favorite soft drink. I didn't eat any of these things, so it was a challenge for me to keep track of them. Inevitably there would be days when one of these essential lunch elements would be missing and he would rant, "I have the same thing for lunch every day, what's so hard about that?"

His anger fueled my resentment. Then I attacked him, complaining about his finicky habits and my having to make a separate trip to the bakery just to buy his special bread. This escalated into more arguments on different subjects.

The more I argued, the more defensive I became and, ironically, the guiltier I felt. I know it sounds silly and non-feminist, but I had just quit my paying job to be a full-time wife and mother, and I really did feel deep down that part of my new duties should be to stock our pantry shelves with 100 percent accuracy.

Finally, one day, I'd had enough. But instead of yelling and screaming and slamming doors and demanding a divorce (as I'd fantasized), I calmly said, "You're right. I *am* a terrible wife because we're out of ham."

A wave of relief washed over me. I let go of my ideas about how I *should* be. I let go of the feeling that I wasn't enough. And I let go of my anger toward my husband.

Then I laughed at the ridiculousness of the whole thing.

Eventually, my husband laughed, too, and decided to take responsibility for his own lunch.

What we resist persists. To be free of an emotion we'd like to get rid of, we must first acknowledge the feeling instead of pretending that it doesn't exist (repressing it) or fighting it. Only then can we release it or simply let it fall away.

⋿ Pray, Let Go, Listen:
Three Steps to Spiritual Surrender

Sometimes (usually when the stakes are low), it's easy to surrender spontaneously. Other times, surrender comes slowly, evolving with the realization that what we're holding onto isn't working, and there must be a better way.

In the middle of writing this book, I was discussing a painful situation that my friend Jody was having with her grown daughter, who was struggling with depression, financial problems, and the stress of being a single mom. Jody had tried everything she could think of to help and support her daughter, but nothing had worked. Her daughter grew only more angry and resentful and finally cut her mother off from her life and the lives of her children—Jody's grandchildren. Jody knew she needed to surrender the situation, but she wasn't sure exactly what to surrender and how to do it. The idea of actually letting go of her daughter terrified her, and she could not give up the hope that there was something she could do. She asked my advice, but I couldn't give her a magic answer. I could only share the process that helps me find my path to spiritual surrender.

This is a good place to point out that ministers, therapists, good friends, and this book can give you guidance, but nobody can tell you exactly *what* or *how* to surrender. There are many possible paths to spiritual surrender, and it is up to each person—with Divine guidance—to determine the right path for him or herself in each situation.

So, how do you discover the surrender that's right for you?

I've found that the following three steps always lead me to my path of surrender, even in the most difficult situations. You don't have to go through these steps to experience spiritual surrender, but they can streamline the process and help you avoid a lot of pain and struggle. The steps are

1. Pray.
2. Let go.
3. Listen.

You don't even have to believe in God to experience spiritual surrender. You must only believe that there is some Higher Power than your rational mind, and trust that this power wants only good for you. You can call that power your intuition, the Universe, the Divine Essence—whatever makes you feel comfortable.

Pray

PRAYER MAY NOT CHANGE THINGS FOR YOU, BUT IT SURE CHANGES YOU FOR THINGS.
—*SAMUEL SHOEMAKER*

Prayer is the medium of miracles, our communication to the Divine. Prayer leads us to the answers we need in our lives, whether we want to hear them or not.

Praying is the first step to conscious surrender. We must quit thinking and instead open ourselves up to a higher realm of knowledge— one beyond the limited expanses of the mind.

Yet we often forget to pray. We *think* with our rational minds, and we can't imagine a way out of our messes. We spend countless hours researching, pondering, brooding, and gathering consensus among our friends about what we should do. We're so busy, we forget to pray, at least until we are really in dire straits. But we need to remember that prayer is not merely the choice of last resort. We can and should pray about all problems and questions in life—no matter how large or how small.

But prayer is not about asking for specific results; it is about acknowledgment and release. We express our problem, situation, or question. We state our intention. We ask for help because we don't know what to do. Thinking hasn't solved our problem.

A powerful prayer is to ask for a shift in *our* perception. "God, please help my husband realize he's being an idiot about this," doesn't work. Instead, we pray, "Please help me to release my fear and anger about this situation. Help me to see only love, and give me the strength to give love and the vision to do your will. Lead me to the path of the greatest good, and walk with me as I travel that path."

Let Go

FATHER, IF IT IS YOUR WILL, TAKE THIS CUP FROM ME; YET NOT MY WILL BUT YOURS BE DONE.
—JESUS, LUKE 22:42

We must give up our will, give up control, and release our expectations about a specific result. This is where the going starts to get tough. We want what we want, and usually we want it yesterday. We need to open ourselves up to the possibility that we don't always know what's best for us.

PRAY NOT FOR LIGHTER BURDENS BUT FOR STRONGER BACKS.
—THEODORE ROOSEVELT

Letting go is especially hard when we're angry. There are times when we feel perfectly entitled to be mad—that anger is the only reasonable solution, and often the world will jump to support us in our anger. This "justified" anger is like a shot of adrenaline, empowering and energizing our egos. And sometimes a burst of anger in just the right place will get things done. Surrender is not about denial or repression. We've got to allow ourselves to feel our emotions completely. Only when we've acknowledged these feelings can we release them. We're human. We're going to feel angry, sad, guilty, jealous—we just can't dwell in these emotions forever.

Whenever I get really mad, I let myself have a little tantrum. I usually call my mother, who's endured her share of foot-stomping and childish behavior after more than four decades of parenting kids. In the safety net of her love, I rant and rave and judge and justify—not at all what I consider spiritually enlightened behavior. Mom usually doesn't disagree or try to solve anything. She just listens, throwing in a few empathetic comments where needed. This goes on until I have exhausted myself. Then I've had enough. When I can't stand to listen to myself anymore, it's time to surrender. Also, I know that if I let the fire of my rage continue to blaze, I'm the one who gets burned—not the object of my wrath, who usually isn't paying any attention to me anyway.

When I can't seem to let go (which is more often than I'd like to admit), there's only one thing to do. I pray for the *willingness* to release my anger. Sometimes I have to pray for this willingness constantly—in the shower, driving the kids to school, unloading the dishwasher—over days or weeks until I feel something inside myself shift—and the rage gradually flicker out. If I'm really, *really* mad, I pray for the willingness to be willing to let go of my anger. This might take some time, but the prayer seems to work on my subconscious. It also works because my conscious mind knows the suffering of holding onto anger is greater than the challenge of letting it go.

Just because we let go of our anger, however, doesn't mean that we can't or shouldn't take action in a situation. Sometimes someone hurts us and it's over and that's it—there's no point in pursuing the matter. If someone cuts us off in traffic, it doesn't do any good to chase them down and confront them—and on some freeways it might get us shot! But if a friend stands us up for a lunch date, or our boss treats us unfairly, or our spouse ignores us at a party and flirts with our best friend, we can and should address these issues. But we'll have a more peaceful and productive encounter if we let go of our anger first and not let it get in the way of what we have to say.

I know that some situations seem impossible or illogical to let go of, but holding onto them is even more irrational. In his book *Forgive for Good,* Dr. Fred Luskin cautions us not to rent too much space in our minds to our grievances. "Focusing too much attention on a hurt makes it stronger and forms a habit that can be difficult to break. You do not have to dwell endlessly on the painful things in your life. Dwelling on wounds gives them power over you," he writes.

Even people who have experienced life's greatest tragedies—the death of a child, physical or sexual abuse, or the Holocaust—have seen the powerful effect in their lives when they are able to let go, accept the past as it happened and life as it is now, and move on.

Elie Wiesel, the Holocaust survivor and Nobel Peace Laureate, has lived through the murder of his parents and unimaginable cruelty and personal suffering, yet he says, "There are moments of anger, others of gratitude, but never of bitterness. To hate would be to reduce myself. Hate destroys the hater as much as his victim."

One might ask, "How can I let go of something so horrible?" Then ask, "How can I not?"

Listen

GOD OFTEN VISITS US, BUT MOST OF THE TIME
WE ARE NOT AT HOME.
—*POLISH PROVERB*

When we pray, we ask for strength and guidance to love, and the wisdom to listen to the answer. With prayer, we invite God into our lives. It's up to us to make sure we're home.

We must trust and then listen carefully to our intuition. The intuitive answer may show up in our hearts as a hunch. We may open a book and find a passage that speaks to us. Some people hear a voice. Sometimes circumstances gently lead us in the direction of the answer. If we don't hear it immediately, we need only ask, and then pay attention; the answer will come.

Usually it's necessary to quiet the chattering inner voices to hear the answer. Traditional meditation is a wonderful way to do this, but it's not the only way. If you are like a lot of people and find it difficult to be still, an active meditation may work better. Going running, pruning the roses, doing Tai Chi, or performing any repetitive motion that doesn't require thought can be a form of meditation. I get some of my greatest bursts of intuition when I am outside jogging, clearing my mind of all thoughts except putting one foot in front of the other and breathing.

Intuition, like surrender, is a word that is often misunderstood. Webster defines *intuition* as "Direct perception of truth, fact, etc., independent of any reasoning process." Intuition is a deep *knowing* that may be based on experience but is not necessarily rooted in any objective facts.

How many times have you felt like you *just knew* something deep within yourself, even though logic may have
contradicted those feelings? Did you trust those feelings or dismiss
them? How did the situation turn out?

Intuition used to be disparaged as only the realm of women back
in the days when that was considered a put-down, or dismissed as
the random guesses of the touchy-feely New Agers. Now intuition
is touted by stock market experts, as well as the spiritually in-tune.

For example, in his book *The New Market Wizards,* Jack D. Schwager
quotes a top trader who describes his use of intuition: "There's buying
and selling going on, but it's just going *through* me. It's like my personality and ego are not there. There's no sense of self at all. There's
just an awareness of what will happen. The trick is to differentiate
between what you *want* to happen and what you *know* will happen.
The intuition *knows* what will happen." The ability to hear our intuition is a power we're all born with—some people have just developed and honored their intuitive power more than others. We may
even be aware of our intuition and just need a little practice opening
ourselves up to hearing it.

LISTENING TO OUR INTUITION

We're surrendering. So we pray, then we let go. Listening is the cru-
cial step when spiritual surrender manifests itself by helping us make
decisions in the real world. Listening is also where things can get
really confusing. While some people can hear and inherently trust
their intuition, most of us believe that intuition is mysterious, available only to the spiritually evolved. It's especially difficult for rational-
minded people, because intuition is so hard to explain or quantify.

Recently I saw a talk show on which a group of intelligent, empow-
ered, spiritual women appeared. Each had given up old careers and
lifestyles that didn't work for them anymore in order to forge new
lives, based upon feelings and intuition.

In front of a rapt audience, the host asked how the women knew when they'd uncovered their intuition, but they just looked blankly at one another. None could provide any guidance other than saying that she "just knew." That's exactly what intuition is—just knowing and then trusting yourself that you know what you know.

For years, I ignored my own intuition in deference to my rational mind, especially when it came to my career.

IT IS THE HEART ALWAYS
THAT SEES, BEFORE THE
HEAD CAN SEE.
—THOMAS CARLYLE

I looked everywhere but inside myself for answers. I spent several years and lots of money seeking advice from therapists, astrologers, and psychics. I bought books like *Follow Your Bliss,* and *Zen and the Art of Making a Living,* and *Do What You Love, and the Money Will Follow*—all to no avail. I was too scared to take that leap into trusting myself; I was sure I was too flaky to be trusted.

In order to follow our intuition, we must first distinguish it from our ego. It's important to make that distinction. After years of listening to my mind, my ego, and everyone else on the planet who was willing to voice an opinion, I began to notice that whenever I went against a "gut" feeling, it always turned out to be a mistake—especially when I used my strength of will to work against my intuition. I can't remember my intuition ever failing me, although I've failed my intuition many times.

For example, in my late twenties, I was laid off from two different sales jobs in the space of two years. Both were large, stable companies that seemed fine one day and were closing down shop the next. Looking back, I realize that was probably a message from the Universe, but the only message I was hearing was from those chattering voices inside my head, saying, "You're a loser."

After my second sudden, devastating plunge into unemployment, I decided to take some time off and decide what I *really* wanted to do for the rest of my life, since this computer sales thing didn't seem to be panning out. Everyone warned me to get busy pounding the pavement, looking for the next job, but I was too dispirited to even try. Against all logic, I took a portion of my meager savings and went off to a cottage by myself where I read, prayed, meditated, took long walks, and soaked in hot pools of mineral water. I didn't talk to anyone except to order a meal or buy a book.

During that period of solitude, I felt reborn. I allowed myself to remember my love of words and telling stories. I specifically remembered one day at the end of my last year of college when I was writing a paper and everything "clicked" and the words just flowed through me. Time stood still, and I felt immense joy and mastery. It was such an exhilarating feeling, such a high, that I didn't want the writing to end. I couldn't recall ever having the same feeling since that day.

I now realize that I "knew" this all along, but I wouldn't allow myself to listen. It was so impractical. All I heard were the rational arguments of my family: "You'll never make any money in writing. It's too competitive," which of course I translated as, "You're not good enough. Don't even bother."

But in my desperation and the stillness of those days after I lost my job, I finally heard my intuition. So after many days of quiet contemplation, I decided to go back to school and get a master's degree in journalism.

I returned home, full of energy and enthusiasm. I studied for the entrance exams, filled out the paperwork, wrote the essays, and even collected recommendations from old professors. I felt alive for the first time in years. This felt totally *right*.

But I didn't follow through. Right before the applications to the programs were due, I got a call out of the blue. My former boss had recommended me for a job. I reluctantly went on the interview, partly out of a sense of gratitude and obligation to my old boss, and partly because the company with the job was headquartered 20 minutes away from where I'd grown up in Virginia and I'd get a free cross-country trip home to see my family. After a quick round of interviews, the company offered me a job where I'd be doing essentially the same thing I'd been doing before—the same thing that I never really liked and had decided I didn't want to do anymore.

I should have walked away from that job, but I couldn't. My rational mind and fear kicked in, beating my intuition to a pulp. What if I turned down this offer and then got rejected from graduate school? Then I'd be left with nothing. Even if I was accepted, I thought about how risky it was to go back to school. How would I pay for everything? I had no idea. What if I couldn't find a job when I got out? Maybe my family was right all along. I thought about the money and security of the new job—the new company guaranteed me a substantial income for a year. I thought about what my family and friends and former coworkers would think if I turned down a lucrative job for the uncertainty of journalism. I "thought" my way into accepting the job and forgetting about graduate school. I listened to my ego and the opinions of everybody else instead of my intuition.

After I accepted the job, I made a couple of weak attempts to satisfy both my intuition and my rational mind. I thought public relations would be a perfect way to segue from sales into writing, so I did a little volunteer PR for a nonprofit organization. But PR wasn't the kind of writing I really wanted to do, and my sales job gave me the excuse of being too busy to pursue anything else, so my writing dreams disappeared onto the back burner for years.

Life eventually brought me back around to my path, but it took more than a decade of struggle in between. I wonder how things might have turned out differently if all those years ago I had followed my intuition—and my true passion—instead of my ego.

IS IT EGO OR INTUITION?

I've learned that truly listening to our intuition involves clearing out the chatter in our heads, including fear, doubts, attack thoughts, vulnerabilities, and general ugliness that often comes to the surface of our mind. These are the voices of the ego.

Not *ego* in the psychotherapy sense of id, ego, and super-ego, and not ego as we traditionally think of blown-up self-esteem, but ego in the sense that we need to believe we are special or better than other people. *A Course in Miracles* describes ego as "quite literally a fearful thought." Our ego is the fear that we are not enough, and it drives us in our desperate struggle to fool the world by proving otherwise. To escape that feeling of worthlessness, we have to make more money, hit the ball farther, have thinner thighs than everyone else—anything to prove that we're not the losers we really believe we are deep down.

That fear drives us to strive manically, to manipulate others, to show off and brag—all to prove our superiority, all to make us feel worthwhile.

Although most people believe that it's good to have a healthy ego, there is nothing healthy about ego in the spiritual sense. Our ego tries to convince us it's there to *serve* and *protect* us. It says, "Where would you be without me? I'm the fire in your belly." But the ego's real ambition is to *separate* us from other people and to keep us away from our true selves.

> YOU BELIEVE THAT WITHOUT THE EGO, ALL WOULD BE CHAOS. YET I ASSURE YOU THAT WITHOUT THE EGO, ALL WOULD BE LOVE.
>
> *A COURSE IN MIRACLES*

We must clear out the ego to be able to hear our intuition—that little voice inside of us that knows what's best for us. But the yelling and screaming and exuberance of the ego often smother that little voice.

The ego is the voice of authority, telling us what we "should" do—not in the sense of moral authority, but in the sense of keeping up appearances and trying to meet other people's expectations. Our intuition is the voice of that playful child, acting out of joy, who has a beginner's mind, believes that anything is possible, and has no fear.

The ego's most powerful weapon is fear. When you quit being afraid, you will be able to hear your intuition. We think that fear, like the ego, protects us. We couldn't be more wrong. Fear only imprisons us.

WHAT IF MY INTUITION IS WRONG?

"But, I've listened to my intuition before and it's been wrong," you think. In these situations, I've found there are two possibilities:

One: We weren't listening to our intuition at all, but rather our ego disguising itself as our intuition. This is tricky. The ego is clever, adaptive, and, like a sociopath, has no conscience and will do anything to have its way. The ego is like the serpent in the Garden of Eden who is described as "more subtle than any beast of the field."

The ego tells us that it's only looking out for our best interests, and that can be a tempting argument. The world has trained us to listen to our egos at the expense of our intuition, so it seems like we're doing the sensible thing when we let our ego be our guide.

So how do you know if you're listening to your ego or your intuition? The key question is

Is the message one of love or fear?

If the message is of love, it's our true self. If it's of fear, it's the ego. Still, sometimes the ego is so insistent and deceptive that we mistake it for our heart.

I once attended a seminar where a woman shared her story of going back to college. She thought she was doing it for herself—listening to her heart. But she quickly discovered she was miserable in college.

Over time she realized she was not going back to school for herself, she was doing it to impress other people. She was making a decision based on the fear of what other people might think of her instead of what her true heart was telling her. She dropped out of college, and is now happily doing something she loves, and it turned out she didn't need the degree after all.

We must pay attention to the signals of the Universe and our own intuition. When we are in tune with ourselves and our Divine purpose, we can use our intuition to stay on the right course, as the automatic pilot on an airplane keeps it going in the right direction. We may veer off course a little here or there but if we keep listening and trusting, we can always correct our path before we get off-course and end up somewhere we don't want to go, or worse—crash and burn.

But what if we believe we hear our intuition, and we're too scared to follow it? We must ask ourselves, "What is the overriding factor: fear or love?"

Are we hesitant to make a change because we love the situation we're in now? Or are we just scared of the unknown?

For example, lots of people stay in bad relationships that they refuse to let go of. Maybe they tell themselves that they love the other person. They want to keep trying to make it work. Or the most self-deceptive, they think they can help the person change by staying in the relationship in spite of their own best interests. Maybe that's what they tell themselves and their friends, but deep down, they're just afraid to leave. They're scared of being alone, scared of failing, scared to think of all the time they've already wasted, or scared to get out there and start all over with someone new. So they stay, despite all the signs screaming for them to leave.

The same thing happens with jobs. There are many people out there in jobs that they know are not right for them. They're not that good at it, they don't really enjoy it, and they feel like they should be doing something different. But they have bills to pay, other people's opinions to worry about, and they're scared to death to try something that they really love because then if they fail, it will really be devastating. It's much easier for people to keep doing something they don't really care about. Then they can always comfort themselves with the thought that it's the job that's making them mediocre—not the other way around.

People all too often wait for the crash—getting dumped from the bad relationship or fired from the dead-end job. Then, when they hit bottom and all else has failed, if they're smart, they start tapping into their intuition. Wouldn't it have been easier to let go of the fear and act earlier—before the crash?

 Don't let fear make your decision for you. Move toward love and away from fear.

Two: The second possibility when we believe our intuition has led us astray is that we *were* listening to our hearts, but the results we had in mind weren't the best thing for us. As Oscar Wilde once wrote, "In this world there are only two tragedies. One is not getting what one wants, and the other is getting it." Perhaps our intuition led us in the perfect direction, even though it wasn't where we wanted to go. Sometimes there's a lesson to be learned in letting go of the outcome. Sometimes God has a more magnificent dream for us than we have for ourselves.

For example, while growing up, college was always a big dream for me, even though I didn't know how I was going to pay for it. So when I looked at colleges, my most important decision factor in selecting a school wasn't the quality of the program (or even the quality of the social life), but how much financial aid I could get. My grades were good enough to apply anywhere I wanted, but I limited myself with my own self-imposed financial constraints, applying only to small schools where I was guaranteed a scholarship. The best "deal" I found was a small, private college that put together a package of scholarships, loans, and a work-study program that exactly equaled the cost of tuition, room, and board.

I loved the school and felt incredibly fortunate. I made friends, joined a sorority, and did well in my classes. Then, my luck changed. My second year, the college raised the tuition, but not the financial aid. I left my minimum-wage work-study job to become a waitress off-campus where I could make enough money to fill the gap and continue going to school.

By my third year, the college had raised tuition again, and I couldn't see how I could possibly come up with enough extra money to return. I cried and I worried and felt completely hopeless. My college dreams that I'd worked so hard to achieve were dissolving in front of my eyes. I wondered how this could be happening and why.

I'm sure I prayed, but I don't remember the words. What I do remember is despondently applying to the University of Virginia, a large, public school where tuition was a fraction of what I'd been paying at the private school. What I didn't realize at the time was what an excellent reputation the university had, and how important that would be in my future.

I was accepted, and during the next two years I had a wonderful time and got a fabulous education—all within my financial means. I graduated with high honors from a university that had a much more prestigious reputation than the smaller college I had originally attended.

While my surrender in this case was more resigned than inspired, this story does illustrate how the Universe sometimes knows what we need better than we know ourselves. And how even if we can't see the outcome, by trusting and continuing to act in a positive way, we can eventually end up in a much better situation.

Beliefs That Hold You Back: Fear, Struggle and Competiton

Fear, struggle, and competition—three concepts that are so deeply ingrained in our culture that we may not even realize the profound impact they have on our lives. These elements lurk in the back of our consciousness, wielding power over our actions, leading us to anxiety, stress, and disconnection from other people. It is only when we shine the light on these self-destructive beliefs, when we bring them into full awareness, that we can see their futility, let them go, and experience miracles.

Surrendering Fear

THERE IS NO FEAR IN LOVE;
BUT PERFECT LOVE CASTETH OUT FEAR.
—1 JOHN 4:18

Most of us live in a state of free-floating fear. Fear is such a part of our everyday existence that we hardly notice it, except when it is extravagantly called to our attention by some horrific news report. The news media's mission seems to be to alert us to all the truly terrifying possibilities in this world, escalating our fears to dramatic proportions. Regardless of what the reality is—crime may be down, the probability of stranger abduction or dying in a plane crash may be infinitesimal—but whenever frightening events occur, they are splashed all over the television and newspaper headlines, making them seem all the more likely and threatening. Children are kidnapped; snipers shoot innocent bystanders, and new studies report that everything we eat causes cancer. Pile all those event-driven fears on top of all our continual anxieties about trying to pay the bills, keep our relationships together, and prove to the world that we're adequate, and we have one big fear-fest.

I should know; I've lived most of my life in fear. I've been afraid of not having enough money, of failure, of being alone, of being made fun of, of being too fat. . . . The list goes on and on. When I think of the regrets I have in my life, they are all things I didn't do because I was too fearful.

Yet the one thing that was *really* terrifying was surrendering my fear. I believed that my fear of failure and fear of being poor motivated me to get out there and make things happen in my life. I'm the first one to admit that fear is a powerful driver. A lot of successful people have got to where they are because of fear.

There's no question that if you're operating out of fear, you may very likely get what you think you want. Our minds create fear, and our minds can be very powerful. But do you really want fear to be your motivator? Is that how you want to live your life? And are the achievements born of fear truly best for us?

> All emotions can be placed into one of two categories: love or fear. Any meaningful action we take is taken out of either love or fear. It is up to each of us to choose which one will guide our life.

Any time we are feeling a "negative" emotion—anger, guilt, sadness, envy, greed—the source is always fear. Fear that someone's putting something over on us. Fear that we didn't do enough. Fear that nobody will love us. Fear that we don't measure up. Fear that we'll never have enough. Whenever you are feeling one of these emotions, ask yourself, "What am I afraid of?" The answer may surprise you.

I don't get angry very often, but when I do—watch out! Sometimes it seems like the smallest provocation can make all hell break loose for me in a seemingly illogical, out-of-proportion way.

Recently my husband took me away for my fortieth birthday to a newly opened luxury hotel. We had Grandma stay with the kids, and we splurged for two glorious nights—a rare treat for us now that we're parents. Almost from the moment we stepped into the hotel, everything seemed to go wrong. It was a holiday weekend, and the hotel did not have our room ready as promised. We had to wait in the crowded bar area of the hotel, which was standing room only. It took forever to get a waiter's attention, and then he brought us the wrong drinks. When we were taken to our room, it was not the ocean view accommodations that we had booked and paid for. We had to go back to the bar to await another room. When we were finally set-tled—hours later—I opened the birthday card from the hotel to find it addressed to not me, but to my husband. That did it and I erupted!

I was on the phone in a flash, demanding to speak to the manager. Luckily he wasn't in and had to call me back, giving me some time to ruminate. I asked myself why I was so furious. It was a new hotel and we were getting a great introductory rate, probably based upon the fact that they didn't have all the kinks worked out yet. My hus-band was slightly annoyed, but seemed to be going with the flow, enjoying the time away with me, whether it was spent in the hotel bar or our room. I asked myself "What am I afraid of?" and the answer was immediately clear.

All this negligence made me feel small, unimportant, and insignif-icant—like the hotel didn't really have to give me the expected level of service because I didn't really deserve it. I felt out of place—like I didn't belong in such a nice hotel. All the feelings of childhood—not having any money, never feeling like I fit in—came flooding back to me. I wasn't angry because my room wasn't ready; I was angry because emotionally I returned to a painful place that I thought I had escaped.

As soon as I realized this, the anger started to melt away. The phone rang and it was the manager, apologizing profusely. I calmly explained our experience. Not in a hostile "How can you do this to me?" kind of a way, but in a "Hey, thought I'd let you know a few things that aren't working quite right yet" kind of way. We had a great conversation and he sent up a bottle of champagne and bought us dinner at the the hotel restaurant the next evening. The rest of the weekend was perfect. I'm not sure if the service in the hotel was any better, but I know my perception of it was healed and that made all the difference. (And the champagne didn't hurt either!)

In every situation, we can choose whether to act out of fear or love. Of course, there's a difference between being fearful and not being stupid. Fear is not what keeps us from running out into the middle of a busy street—common sense takes care of that. Running into the path of a Mack truck is not an act of love and fearlessness—it's recklessness.

Some of the people who seem on the surface to be the most fearless are, in fact, the most driven by fear. These people may take dangerous chances and perform outrageous stunts, solely out of a desire to make themselves appear special, when they are really motivated by the fear of their own ego. Fear and ego are perfect soul mates.

So how do you release fear? Acknowledge it and face it. First realize that fear is the source of hostility, jealousy, guilt, feelings of inadequacy, and a whole bunch of emotions that make us feel bad. Make it a habit to ask yourself, "What am I afraid of in this situation?" Acknowledge your answer. Then, whatever it is, go forward and act out of love instead of fear. Awareness is more than half the process. With awareness, the fear will gradually melt away—maybe not all at once, but little by little until you notice that you are not nearly as scared as you used to be. It's taken a lifetime to become this fearful, and it will take some time to learn to recognize it and let it go. Trust in the process and it will happen.

Once we begin to acknowledge and release our fear, we can hear our intuition. Then we must have the faith to believe in it, trust it, and follow through on its message.

Surrendering the Struggle

WHEN WE HARNESS THE FORCES OF HARMONY, JOY, AND LOVE, WE CREATE SUCCESS AND GOOD FORTUNE WITH EFFORTLESS EASE.
—DEEPAK CHOPRA,
THE SEVEN SPIRITUAL LAWS OF SUCCESS

Conventional wisdom has always decreed that life is difficult. "You're not supposed to like your job—that's why it's called work," I remember my father saying.

But the truth is, conventional wisdom is wrong. We don't need to struggle. We can relax, surrender to a Higher Power, and let our destinies unfold perfectly.

When you pray, let go, and listen, the answer may not be what you expect or what you want to hear, but the answer will *not* be a struggle. It will feel right and move you toward your greatest potential, whereas struggle is a negative force that moves you away from something—making you resist.

> WE COME TO GOD BY LOVE AND NOT BY NAVIGATION.
> —SAINT AUGUSTINE

In most situations, you can determine if something is a struggle by adding the word *against* after *struggle*. If you are struggling *against* something, take another look at the situation. Is it possible to move *toward* something positive instead? The difference between the two may seem subtle, but it can completely affect your attitude and actions.

My old job selling software is a perfect example. In sales, you can struggle and fight against the competition, or you can act out of love and service to the customer. Regardless of the outcome, the difference between the two approaches is peace of mind.

Once you've surrendered, you may still need to put in some old-fashioned hard work, but it will feel right. You will be acting from a place of love, not fear or ego.

Here's an early example of how I gave up a futile struggle and learned to flow with a natural force of life. The summer I turned fifteen, my best friend, Trish, and her mom took me along for their annual vacation at Virginia Beach. I had never before been to the beach or seen the ocean, and I was beside myself with excitement.

We arrived on a sweltering August afternoon, and we couldn't wait to hit the water. Trish ran into the surf and called for me to follow. I started cautiously at first, and then rushed in deeper to catch up with my friend.

Suddenly, an enormous wave knocked me down. I panicked. This was a different experience. I wasn't a great swimmer, and I'd only swum in pools before. Disoriented, I struggled, fighting the tide to get my head above water. The instant I succeeded, another wave barreled over me, pulling me under the water again, tossing me about, salt water and sand in my eyes and nose, everything a big confusing jumble. Just when I was sure I would drown, I discovered that the waves had brought me back to a shallow area where I was safe.

Later I learned the art of bodysurfing—letting my body flow with the waves, instead of fighting them. I learned that if I relaxed into the waves, the ocean would always bring me safely back to the shore.

God, the Universe, is the ocean that will bring us safely home in any situation.

This is hard to believe when we're in pain. Nobody can explain why terrible things happen to nice people. Nobody knows what is in God's mind when someone we love dies or when a senseless tragedy occurs.

What we *can* understand is that resisting and struggling makes our hardships even more difficult. The process of overcoming grief may be long and varied, but it always ends with acceptance.

SURRENDER IN ACTION

Just as spiritual surrender is not passive, releasing the struggle does not mean that we never have to "fight." For example, if anyone tries to harm my children, I'll fight like a mother bear to protect them. And while politically I'm more of a dove than a hawk, I believe there are times when a nation must fight to keep innocent people safe from harm. The core motivation of these actions must be the desire to maintain peace rather than pure aggression and ego. We take action because we love what we are protecting—our children, our people, our freedom, and once they're safe, we stop fighting. We must keep checking our internal barometer of intuition to make sure that our action always feels right—that our source is always love.

A memorable example of this concept is the action of the passengers on United Flight 93 on September 11, 2001. When they discovered that three other hi-jacked planes had intentionally been crashed into buildings, killing thousands of innocent people, they decided to take action and try to reclaim the plane from the terrorists.

In particular, Todd Beamer, one of the leaders of the revolt against the terrorists, exemplified the strength of surrender—of taking action and then letting go. As his wife, Lisa, describes in her book, *Let's Roll:*

> *While his final actions did require great courage, something else he did that morning required even more. In the face of the worst circumstances he could humanly imagine, Todd chose to rest in the words of the Lord's Prayer: "Thy will be done." He put himself in the hands of God, knowing that ultimately that was the only safe place to be. Of course Todd wanted to come home on September 11, but he knew if that didn't happen, God was still in control and would take care of him and us.*

As the prayer continues, "And forgive us our trespasses, as we forgive those who trespass against us," Lisa said that she believed her husband was forgiving the terrorists. The action that those passengers took required them to give up their fear of their own injury or death and act for a greater good, resulting in the plane crashing in a barren Pennsylvania field instead of into a major center like the White House or the Capitol. Their action saved hundreds, or perhaps even thousands, of lives and gave America a measure of hope on our darkest day in modern history. Todd Beamer's decision to recite the Lord's Prayer as one of his last acts is an incredible example of surrendering fear, and taking heroic action in the midst of chaos and tragedy.

Surrendering Competition

COMPARISON MUST BE AN EGO DEVICE,
FOR LOVE MAKES NONE.
A COURSE IN MIRACLES

A big part of surrendering the struggle is letting go of the idea that everything in life is a competition—a real challenge in a culture that thrives on competition and idolizes winners.

We all want to succeed. However, constantly competing can actually get in the way of achieving our dreams and separate us from other people. We all know people who have to be the best—whether it's at work, making money in the stock market, or by having the smartest kids. Instead of being admired, as they desire, those people are usually avoided. Not because others are jealous, but because these people's obsession with winning disconnects them from other people in their world. They must win, and therefore, everyone else must lose—not a very compelling foundation for a relationship.

The idea of competition is based on the "scarcity mindset"—that there's only so much to go around, so I'd better grab my share. This thinking is bound to manifest lack in our lives. If we believe that there is never enough, there never will be—no matter how much we have.

Believing that the world is big enough for everyone's success opens up the opportunities for our own success. Like attracts like, so when we act in a loving, giving manner—without thoughts of competition or expectations for what we will get—we naturally become a magnet for other people's generosity and good things to flow to us.

I once had a writing teacher, Kelly, who, among her many accomplishments, wrote a book about boomerangs. All her students love Kelly, as she always gives much more than one would expect from an instructor. She balances a family, a couple of jobs, and a freelance writing career, but she is always willing to go the extra mile for her students. She's had great success and some incredible opportunities open up for her. Kelly is a living example of her "Boomerang Philosophy," which says that you throw out good things and good things come back to you. But she adds, "If you put strings on it or weight it down with expectations, it doesn't come back."

I recently had a boomerang experience. One Saturday morning I opened up the book section of the newspaper and read an article about a Silicon Valley author who had published a new book—a collection of essays about discovering spirituality in the craziness of her daily life of raising kids.

I'm ashamed to admit my first reaction was not, "Great! What a delightful book. I must rush out and buy it." Instead, I thought, "Damn! That's the book I wanted to write! She beat me to it!"

Of course, this is a completely insane reaction. There are several books on the shelves about finding spiritual lessons in motherhood, and there's bound to be plenty of room for more in the future. But that didn't stop my ego from jumping in there with its own paranoid delusions: Now that she's written this book, I'll never be able to get mine published. What if her book is better than anything I could write? I should have acted as soon as I got the idea; now the opportunity is lost for me. And more crazy, chattering, drama queen voices— belittling myself, envying her, and bemoaning the unfairness of it all.

Then an amazing thing happened. Within the week, the author of spiritual/mothering book contacted *me* through my website. She was warm, funny, charming, and we had a lot in common besides our spiritual inclinations and our seven-year-old daughters. We continued an e-mail correspondence, and she told me that she was coming to my city to do a book signing at one of the local bookstores. Since I freelance for the local paper, I offered to write an article to promote her event. I thought it would be a fun story, applicable to the family-oriented city where I live, and would help her sell a few books, too. By this time I liked this author so much that I was able to forget about my envy at her having stolen my idea.

I worked especially hard on the article, putting in many more hours than usual to get it just right. The author came to town, we met for dinner, and then I attended her book signing. I had also sent e-mails inviting other mothers and/or writers I knew to the event, and I sat with an acquaintance who knew about my spiritual surrender book. During her talk, the author generously introduced me as the writer of the article that drew many of the people in the audience to the talk, and mentioned that I was writing a book, too.

Later, as the author signed books, my friend and I were discussing spiritual surrender on the way to the café for coffee. "But I just don't understand," said my friend. "How can you surrender and still make things happen in your life?"

I didn't have a chance to answer. At that very moment, a smiling woman approached me, extending her hand and her business card. "I'm the regional events manager for (this national book store chain)," she said. "I loved your article. When your book is out, call me about setting up book signings in all our stores." But wait; it gets better.

As we talked about the subject of my book, I discovered that in addition to being a very influential person in a large chain of bookstores, this woman was also a longtime student of *A Course in Miracles*. The more we talked, the more we clicked, and I ended up feeling that I'd found a new best friend.

When she finally had to excuse herself to wrap up the event, the friend who had joined me at the event said, in wide-eyed amazement, "You don't have to answer my question. I think I get it."

I got it, too, and it was a wonderful lesson. By releasing my initial response of fear, scarcity, and competition, I was able to give my help joyfully, make new friends, have fun, and open the door to a wonderful opportunity. My generosity boomeranged right back to me—multiplied many times over in a way that I never could have envisioned.

Keep Your Dreams, Lose Your Expectations: Intentions, Goals, and Results

> *If you want to make God laugh, make a plan—or stubbornly hang onto your idea of how the plan should manifest.*

So surrender sounds like the spiritually right thing to do, but maybe you're afraid it will mean a life of boredom or poverty. One of the biggest problems I originally had with spiritual surrender was letting go of my goals. Goals were my friends. They had served me well. I'd always considered myself "goal-oriented," which I thought was an admirable quality. I couldn't imagine a life without goals.

Without them, I believed I would drift along aimlessly just waiting for my life to happen to me. I know people who have taken this approach to spiritual surrender. Their attitude was, "God will take care of me," but the subtext of their belief seemed to be, "so *I* don't have to do anything."

For example, I have a friend who lost her job but didn't bother looking for a new one—sure that God would lead her to the perfect position. While she waited patiently for her sign from God, she lost her house, had to sell all her possessions, eventually couldn't pay her bills, and went bankrupt. I'm not being sarcastic when I say that maybe that was her spiritual path, but I knew it wasn't mine.

An old Indian proverb says, "Call on God, but row away from the rocks."

> Spiritual surrender is not about doing nothing. It is about releasing what's not working in our lives, asking for guidance, and opening ourselves up to the opportunities that come our way, then acting on them.

There's an often-told story of a devoutly religious man who was caught in a flood. He climbed to the roof of his house and prayed to God to be saved. A raft, a rowboat, and a helicopter tried to rescue him, but he rebuffed them all, saying he was waiting for God. The water continued to rise and, eventually, the man drowned. When he met God in heaven, the man was really ticked off. "I trusted you," he said. "I put all my faith in you. Where were you? Why didn't you save me?"

God replied, "I sent you a raft, a rowboat, and a helicopter. What more did you want me to do?"

How many times have we called on God and then ignored the opportunities he sent? Maybe we didn't recognize them because they didn't take the form we expected. Spiritual surrender requires faith, but it also requires paying attention to opportunities and taking action. We need to look to God for guidance, to keep us on the right course, but we can't expect God to kick-start us every morning and deliver breakfast in bed.

My great "Aha!" moment regarding spiritual surrender came when I realized I didn't have to give up my dreams to live a surrendered life. I could keep my dreams but release my *attachment* to the results. At first blush, this might sound contradictory, but when examined more deeply, it makes the whole concept of practicing spiritual surrender come together.

GOD GIVES EVERY BIRD ITS FOOD, BUT HE DOES NOT THROW IT INTO THE NEST.
—J. G. HOLLAND

The key to this apparent paradox is the difference among *intentions*, *goals*, and *results*, and understanding how they work within the context of spiritual surrender.

Intentions

An *intention* is always the beginning:

> Intention is what we would like to see happen in our life. We create the intention, and then we start to move in that direction. Having the intention out there (in the Universe) and in here (in our heads and hearts) helps us move toward our Divine destiny.

We must take our intentions very seriously, and make sure they are truly what we desire, not just what we think we *should* desire, or what someone else has told us that we should desire.

Barbara Sher's book, *I Could Do Anything If I Only Knew What It Was,* discusses the concept of a "touchstone," which is the element "at the heart of what you love to do. Your touchstone is the delicious core of all the things you want—the part that makes them truly appealing to you."

We may think our dreams are impossible, and they may be impractical considering our physical, financial, or family constraints. But our *touchstone* is always within our reach and honoring it is essential for a feeling of purpose and fulfillment. For example, if you always dreamed of being a prima ballerina, and now you're middle-aged, the natural forces of age and gravity may keep you from achieving that specific dream. However, your touchstone is not as narrowly defined as your fantasy. If you really think about why you want to be a prima ballerina, you'll probably discover different, broader touchstones that are entirely within your grasp.

Your touchstones may be the enjoyment of dancing, the feeling of being on center stage, or creatively working in music—and these dreams are possible at any age. Instead of becoming a prima ballerina, you may teach dance classes, act in community theater, or create performance art to the accompaniment of *Swan Lake*. Once you let go of your limited idea of your dream, endless possibilities emerge for achieving it.

A touchstone is to a dream what an intention is to a goal—a bigger, more robust version of what you think will make you happy. Intentions, like touchstones, are based upon true joy—not ego or someone else's expectations. A touchstone or an intention leaves itself open to more possibilities than do mere dreams or goals. Finding the touchstone of our dreams helps us develop intentions, which enable us to set a course and navigate through the many decisions and obstacles in life.

Going through life with no dreams or intentions is not spiritual—it's wasting your potential. You need to have a reason for getting out of bed in the morning, and you'll be happier if you're aware of your intentions and you choose them wisely. Your intention doesn't have to be material or selfish, however; it may be as simple as to live your life every day in a loving way or may be as vast as working toward world peace.

Think of an intention as the beginning of a journey. Let's say you want to go someplace sunny and warm near the water—that's your intention, and it will guide you to your ultimate destination, which could be Miami Beach, Honolulu, or an island in Fiji.

Focus on your intentions and not on the limiting circumstances surrounding you. Your intention may be to have a happy marriage. Maybe it will be with your current boyfriend or girlfriend, husband or wife, or maybe not. After releasing your fear and anger, and acting with love in your relationship, you may find this relationship will never evolve into the happy marriage of your dreams. Then you need either to realize your intention elsewhere or to change your intention. The important thing is to be aware of your decisions and act always toward your true intentions, instead of making excuses or clinging to a situation that is a lost cause.

Again, ask yourself, "Am I acting out of love or fear?" Let the answer be your guide.

Goals

A *goal* is the next step after an intention has been created:

Goals are how we would like to see our particular intention manifested. Surrender begins when we release our goals, and open ourselves up to receiving them or something better.

The concept of goals has been trumpeted as the secret to success in school, work, and relationships, especially over the past couple of decades. Like most people of my generation, I learned that "there is magic in goals." I was taught to write my goals down, clearly define them, and make them objective with time limits ("I will win the Nobel Prize by 2010," or "I will survive breast-feeding for six months") and reasonable (not, "I will sprout wings and fly" or "I will convince my husband to put his dirty dishes in the dishwasher"). I learned that if I followed all the rules, I could meet my goals, and I still believe this is true. But, now, I'm not so sure I really want to achieve all my goals—at least not exactly the way I might envision them.

In the book *Living Without a Goal*, James Ogilvy says,

> [Living without a goal] is about designing life artistically rather than engineering life mechanically. Artistic design calls for freedom and spontaneity where engineering builds upon the laws of mechanical necessity. Many of us use Grand Goals to deny our own freedom. We allow ourselves to become the slaves of our Goals. You know the story. Get up in the morning. Go to work. You confront the tasks in front of you. You experience each moment as a means to the next. One job leads to another. You become tools of your tasks. This is slavery, not freedom.

Goals can be valuable as markers or milestones, like the signs on the highway that tell us how far we've traveled and how far we have yet to go on our journey. But we should be careful not to get too attached to them. There may be obstacles along the way that are out of our control—like mechanical breakdowns, traffic jams, or accidents. Or we may decide to take a scenic detour that delays our arrival at the destination, but makes the trip a lot more fun.

The idea of not being attached to goals may seem contrary to conventional wisdom, which tells us to make a goal and stick to it, come hell or high water. That approach might mean that we accomplish our goal, but what good is the achievement if we end up in hell or drowning?

Results

The last leg of the journey is *results* or "outcomes":

Results are specifically what we want to happen. Results are the physical forms, like Miami Beach, or a red Mercedes convertible or a husband who is tall, dark, handsome, and rich.

One of the most miraculous things about spiritual surrender is realizing how misguided we may be in defining specific results. The outcomes we imagine may not be what we actually need, or may not be the best thing for us in the long run. Miami Beach may be too crowded. The red convertible may attract too much attention from the highway patrol, and we'll end up with lots of speeding tickets. The handsome husband (or beautiful wife) may be selfish or abusive or cheat on us.

Gandhi, who achieved an almost inconceivably impossible result—freeing his country from British imperial rule through peaceful resistance—said this when asked the secret of his life in three words: "Renounce and enjoy!", meaning that to enjoy life, we must not be attached to anything. He added, "By detachment I mean that you must not worry whether the desired result follows from your action or not, so long as your

motive is pure, your means correct. Really, it means that things
will come right in the end if you take care of the means and leave
the rest to him."

Too often the results we are striving for don't originate within ourselves, but come from parents, the media, or other external influences.
These messages can become so ingrained within us that we don't
even realize they are not ours.

One day when I was in my twenties and working myself to exhaus-
tion, I saw an image at a street fair that I'll never forget. It was a draw-
ing of a cat, all scrunched up and looking quite miserable and helpless
in the bottom of a long-necked bottle. The caption read, "The cat
who worked very, very, very hard to get inside of a bottle and now
can't remember why."

To my dismay, I realized that cat was me.

I can recall so many times in my life when I have strictly defined
and struggled toward results that ended up not being what I wanted
or needed at all. Often, my blind pursuit of my own version of *what
I thought I had to have* got in the way of a much better outcome. We
think we know exactly what we want, precisely what will make us
happy, but often our rational mind gets it all wrong. Sometimes our
dreams can even be too small, too limiting—God may have a grander
plan for us.

By forming intentions, being flexible with our goals, and surrendering our results, we work together with the Universe to create a
beautiful and unique life with a free hand, instead of forcing ourselves always to color between the lines.

When I started writing this book, I was continually frustrated. I
already had a more-than-full-time job of being a stay-at-home mother
to my two small children. I was also freelancing for the local newspaper, a job that I loved and could squeeze in around brief nap-
times and preschool, and in the early, early mornings before the
kids woke up.

It quickly became obvious that I couldn't cram writing a book
into the already stretched-to-the-limits constraints of my life. Writ-

ing a book required big chunks of time in which to think, dream, and create—not stolen snatches of time here and there.

I decided, in my most ambitiously optimistic frame of mind, that one full day a week (with no interruptions) would be enough for me to make significant progress on the book and still take sufficient care of everyone else.

My *intention* was to have time to write the book. My *goal* then became to find a part-time nanny who could work one weekday from 9 to 5. The way I pictured this nanny, my *result*, was a loving young college student (maybe one who was studying early child-hood development) who would come in one day a week and completely take care of the kids for eight hours.

Thus began my two-month fruitless search. I ran ads in the newspaper, asked friends and strangers, and everything else my rational mind could conceive. And, of course, I prayed.

No young college student appeared.

But something better happened. My husband, a hard-working entrepreneur who generally left most of the responsibility for the kids to me, said he would take the kids and do something fun with them on Sundays so I could write.

Bingo! Not only had I wanted time to write, but also I'd long been frustrated that my husband wasn't spending more time with the kids. My husband often said he felt left out in our family—standing just outside of the tight emotional triad that the kids and I shared. Even so, it never crossed my mind to ask him to take care of the kids one day a week so I could work on this book. I thought he would think the book was a silly pursuit, and he'd resist being responsible for the kids for a whole day by himself. When he volunteered, I got my intention, but with a totally unexpected outcome that was better than anything I could have imagined! His support and his belief in me strengthened our relationship. The time he has spent with the kids has resulted in the three of them becoming much closer than they've ever been. And I got to follow my dream and write this book.

We can live a surrendered life, and continue to move toward our dreams, if we remember these elements:

1. Create an intention.
2. Let go of preconceived ideas of how the intention will manifest.
3. Take action—always from love, not fear.
4. Work hard, but do not "struggle against."
5. Pay attention to your intuition—to both the synchronicities and the unease that you encounter—to help you stay on the right course.
6. Go with the flow and trust in the wisdom and benevolence of a Higher Power.

The Four Types of Surrender

We hear the words *surrender, release,* and *letting go* bantered about all the time, as if they all mean the same thing. Spiritual surrender is easier to comprehend and practice when we break it down into the following four types: Letting Go, Surrendering a Problem, Going with the Flow, and Surrendering to Love. The following chapters explain these concepts and tell the stories of how people facing life's difficulties experienced these different types of surrender.

letting go

ONE OF THE MOST POWERFUL TEACHINGS OF THE BUDDHIST
TRADITION IS THAT AS LONG AS YOU ARE WISHING FOR THINGS
TO CHANGE, THEY NEVER WILL.

—PEMA CHÖDRÖN, *START WHERE YOU ARE*

THE FIRST TYPE of surrender is letting go of what
isn't working in our lives, whether it's painful feelings, limiting beliefs, or situations that we need to release.

Anger, fear, resentment, guilt, and jealousy are some of the emotions we harbor—or even nurture—that eat away at our peace of
mind and our happiness. Why not decide to let them go?

The belief that we need to be perfect, or that life has to be a struggle, or that nobody will ever love us are some of the beliefs that pre-
vent us from being happy and hold us back from realizing our greatest
potential. We know in our hearts and our minds that these beliefs
don't serve us, so why do we hang onto them?

We may know that we need to let go of an abusive relationship,
a dead-end job, or our expectations of our spouse, children, or mother-
in-law, but feel paralyzed to change. Why do we feel so stuck in bad
situations?

If letting go is hard for you, you're not alone. People are generally
much more motivated by fear of loss than by the potential of gain.
Every experienced salesperson knows this, and that's why we so often
see the FUD (fear, uncertainty, and doubt) sales pitch, as in, "You
must act now! Limited time offer!" The idea is that we'll be so scared
we'll miss out and lose the opportunity that we'll act right away.

Another example is to ask, "Which scenario would make you work harder?" The possibility of losing $1,000 you have in the bank now, or the opportunity to earn $1,000? If you're like most people, you'd work much harder to avoid losing money you already have.

We are conditioned to fear loss, and that fear carries through much of our lives—even when it doesn't make any sense. It explains why we hang onto clothes in the closet that we know we'll never fit into again or a miserable marriage that never gets any better. We cling to the old and familiar, even if we know it's not doing us any good. It's like the old saying, "The devil you know is better than the devil you don't."

If we decide to let go of our fear, we will discover that releasing the negative in our lives makes room for the positive—like love, serendipity, and abundance.

For example, I'm always packing stuff away to donate to charities and homeless shelters, yet I used to find that I still had a closetful of old clothes that were outdated, didn't fit, or were perfectly good, but I was just tired of wearing. I just couldn't make myself part with them. I knew that some kind of deep-seated, unreasonable fear was compelling me to hold onto stuff I didn't want or need, but being aware of it didn't make it any easier to overcome.

One day I was browsing in my favorite store and feeling more than a little guilty about the possibility of buying anything new with all the old clothes languishing in my closet. I admitted this to the salesperson, and she gave me a wonderful idea. She told me that every time she buys something new, she gives away something in her closet. This way her closets don't get too full, and someone else benefits from her new purchase. This keeps "the flow" moving.

I made a rule to do the same, and now, whenever I buy something new, I immediately go home and make a giveaway pile of at least one old thing for each new thing I purchased. Getting rid of the old makes room for the new, whether in our bedroom closets or our spiritual closets.

Letting go has to truly happen in our heart and souls, not just for appearances. You can magnanimously tell everyone, "Oh, yes, I've forgiven my ex-husband," while you're mentally replaying every time he cheated on you. You can say, "I don't need money to be happy," while you're buying lottery tickets or envying your neighbor's new Lexus, but you're not convincing anyone—not even yourself. You can't merely pretend to let go, thinking that you can trick the Universe into giving you what you actually want if you act like you don't care.

One of the funniest, truest lines in *Bridget Jones's Diary* was her New Year's resolution to not "sulk about having no boyfriend, but develop inner poise and authority and sense of self as woman of substance, complete without boyfriend, as best way to obtain boyfriend." If you've ever tried this, you know it is not letting go (and it probably won't work anyway).

Acceptance and Forgiveness

Two major aspects of letting go are *acceptance* and *forgiveness.*

Acceptance of the way things are enables us to give up struggling and relax into the Divine flow of life. A wise friend once told me that whenever we're caught in the belief that things should be different (better) than they are, we're not "in acceptance," which cuts off abundance in our lives.

Acceptance is letting go of our expectations about how things *should* be and appreciating what is.

In her book *Loving What Is,* Byron Katie tells us, "The only time we suffer is when we believe a thought that argues with what is. . . . When we argue with (reality), we experience tension and frustration. We don't feel natural or balanced. When we stop opposing reality, action becomes simple, fluid, kind, and fearless."

A step beyond acceptance is gratitude. When we're practicing gratitude, we not only stop denying and resisting what is; we recognize the blessings inherent in each situation. As M.J. Ryan says in her book *Attitudes of Gratitude,* "Gratitude helps us to return to our natural state of joyfulness where we notice what's right instead of what's wrong. Gratitude births only positive feelings—love, compassion, joy, and hope. As we focus on what we are thankful for, fear, anger, and bitterness simply melt away, seemingly without effort." Acceptance and gratitude are just a matter of perspective. Changing the way we think can change our life in an instant, opening the door for miracles.

For example, with my first baby, I couldn't wait for her to go to sleep each night. She was so demanding, so energetic, and she needed such little sleep that I felt like I never had a free minute. I kept telling myself, "She *should* be sleeping more," and gathering evidence to support my case by reading books on sleep and comparing her sleeping habits to friends' babies. The cold, hard facts of typical baby sleeping behavior had no influence on her; apparently it didn't bother her that she was at the end of the "normal" bell curve.

I tried suggestions from family, friends, and pediatricians—all to no avail. I was heavily into denial and resistance and thought there must be some secret tactic that I was missing. Bedtime was always a struggle, and I left her room the moment she fell asleep. Then, when she finally did sleep, I couldn't enjoy it—I was so anxious about when she would wake up and start the whole cycle again!

Now, with my second child, I have a different outlook. After seven years of motherhood, I realize there are a lot of things about children that *just are* and can't be changed or controlled—including each child's inherent need for sleep. Some kids need a lot of sleep and some kids need only a little. I accept this now—and thank God that my son tends more toward normal in this respect.

But I've moved beyond acceptance and into gratitude for the time I spend putting my son to sleep. It might be spiritual growth on my part, but it's just as likely that my change of attitude is because he's my last baby and I want to cherish every second of my time with him. Either way, I'll take progress however it happens.

Every night he and I have the same ritual. We crawl into the bottom bunk of his bed, curl up under the covers, and I ask him what kind of a story he wants—scary or friendly? About dinosaurs or dragons? Then we snuggle and I pat his head and weave an imaginary tale just for him. Gradually his eyes become heavy and his breathing becomes deep. Sometimes he makes a little boy snoring sound. And when he's finally asleep, I don't jump up and out of his room; I linger. I touch his cheeks and take in the smell of baby shampoo in his hair. And every night, in the quiet of his room, I say a prayer and thank God for my beautiful children and all the other blessings in my life. The end of my day is no longer a struggle; it's a moment of peace and joy and gratitude—a miracle in my life.

Miracles are born of forgiveness—of letting go of the hurts, anger, and bitterness that we store up inside ourselves when we've been wronged. We may need to forgive others or we may need to forgive ourselves—both free us and lighten our burdens.

There's a common misperception that to forgive someone means letting them off the hook, and that we must feel the same way about them and act the same way as we treated them before—forgive and forget. This is not necessarily the case.

If you're forgiving someone with whom you have a close relationship that you want to keep—like your husband, for instance—forgiving and forgetting is the best policy. As Marlene Dietrich said, "Once a woman has forgiven her man, she must not reheat his sins for breakfast."

But forgiveness doesn't mean that we have to think the person who wronged us is right, or even that we have to continue to be friends. We won't necessarily want to be friends with everyone we forgive, and they won't necessarily want to be friends with us. Forgiveness just means that we let go of the anger and the resentment and the "if only" thoughts that tear us up inside. Simply put, forgiveness is giving up the hope that the past could have been any different.

Some people have difficulties with forgiveness because they think it makes them a doormat, and they don't want the offender to "get away with" something. This, of course, is completely absurd, because most of the times we harbor anger and grudges, the object of our wrath couldn't care less—making us even more angry, frustrated, and determined not to forgive. So who's really hurt when we resist forgiveness?

Dr. Fred Luskin, author of *Forgive for Good,* conducts forgiveness workshops at Stanford University. Over the years, he has helped people with all types of grievances to forgive, including families of victims of the conflict in Northern Ireland. In his research, he has found that people who forgive have less stress, cardiovascular disease, and cancer, and feel better psychologically and emotionally. Why should we let someone who hurt us once continue to hurt us by our own stubborn refusal to forgive? Letting go of anger and embracing forgiveness is one of the most fundamental examples of spiritual surrender.

The most difficult time I ever had forgiving was when my best friend, and maid of honor, "Lauren," broke off all ties with me—without any explanation—three months before my wedding. I only have brothers, and Lauren felt like the sister I'd always wanted but never had. We became friends when we were both single career girls in San Francisco, and we'd been through boyfriends and heartbreaks, promotions and lousy bosses, earthquakes, and even Paris together. We knew that we could always count on each other whenever work, family, or men failed us—which was often.

When she got married, she asked me to be her maid of honor. Two years later, when I became engaged, I chose her to be mine. But as the date approached, she kept canceling dates for her dress fitting. I knew something was wrong, but she denied it. Then, one day, she just quit calling me or taking my phone calls altogether. I was baffled. I called her sister, I wrote Lauren a letter, I stopped by her house, but she was never home. I finally reached her on the phone, but she said she was busy and she'd call me back, but she never did. I was as heartbroken as I would have been if my fiancé had dumped me—after all, Lauren and I had been together longer, and we'd been through more. I cried for weeks and wondered what I could have possibly done to make her act like this.

Then, one day much later, after many tears and prayers, I accepted the fact that our friendship was over. I couldn't think of anything I could do to change her mind, and (as Dr. Luskin would say) I was tired of renting out so much space to her in my head. So I prayed for the willingness to forgive, and then I prayed for the forgiveness to come, and eventually it did. I forgave Lauren for ditching our years-long friendship without explanation, and—just as important—I forgave myself. I quit beating myself up and wondering what I'd done wrong—Had I been impatient? Thoughtless? Did she hate the bridesmaid dress I picked?—and I knew that no amount of anger or hurt or wishing things could be different would change anything.

There was no tangible magic to the experience—Lauren didn't immediately "see the light" and come running back apologizing to me, and I haven't seen her since. I still don't know why she ended the friendship, and I've quit trying to figure it out. I still feel sad when I think about it, which is not so much anymore. Whenever I do run across old photos of us stashed away in albums, mostly I have happy thoughts of our friendship and our times together. The rest, I let go.

Forgiveness is about acceptance. Forgiveness can't erase all hurt, and that's just the way things are sometimes. We accept our sadness and our wounds. But it's our choice whether we let that hurt control us, or if we acknowledge it and then let it go. Letting it go is the only way to reclaim the peace in our lives.

The Perfect Girlfriend

DEEP WITHIN YOU IS EVERYTHING THAT IS PERFECT, READY TO
RADIATE THROUGH YOU AND OUT INTO THE WORLD.
—*A COURSE IN MIRACLES*

TONY AND I had been together for three years. It took me only three dates to know—without a doubt in my mind—that he was the one for me. I'd never even thought about getting married until I met Tony, but by that third date I knew, and after that, I was just waiting for him to realize it too.

It took him much longer.

Even though he didn't share my enthusiasm, our relationship continued and I remained happy with Tony. I thought it would have been romantic if he had realized how right we were for each other straight away, but I didn't hold it against him. I just carried on being the right kind of girlfriend, believing eventually I could convince him of what I already knew.

Every birthday, every Valentine's Day, every Christmas, and every New Year's, I would silently hope he would pull out that ring for me. When he would say he was getting me something "very, very special," my heart would do a little leap. As nice as the presents were, though, they were never that engagement ring I was hoping for. Part of me hated myself for being so disappointed at such lovely, thoughtful presents, but another part became even more determined to prove that I was the right girl for him.

At about the two-year mark, things changed. I could no longer stand the waiting. I had told myself I would never be the type of girl who would hound her man about marriage, but that's exactly what I did. It started with little hints.

A married couple would come over for dinner, and after they left I would say, "It must be nice to have a real commitment to someone." We would be at a movie and someone in the film would get engaged. "She must be so happy," I would say. We would see a man in the park playing with his kids. "I think you'll make a wonderful father," I would say. I'd see an ad for a psychic on television. "Maybe I'll call her," I would say. "I'd like to know our future."

"Why do you need to know the future?" he asked. "We're happy now, isn't that enough?"

"I don't know if that's enough."

"Why not? I'm with you. I like you. I'm not going to leave you."

"Ever?"

"Why do you have to push these things all the time?"

"I'm not pushing, I'm just asking."

"It's not your job to ask, it's mine."

"But will you ever ask?"

"Stop pushing."

Those little hints and harmless comments turned into major arguments.

"I don't understand," I would say through tears.

"I'm just not ready."

"You've known me for two years. If you don't love me enough now, when are you ever going to?"

"I just don't know."

"But I do everything right."

"You do," he said. "You've always been a good girlfriend."

"What more do you need from me?"

That was the big question to which I needed an answer. But he had no answer.

"How long can I wait?" I asked myself. "If he doesn't love me now, he never will. I have to accept that and let him go." But it was always just too hard to let go.

It was the night we went out to dinner with his friends that I decided. Tony was a soldier, and there had been recent talk of him being sent away to war. I never believed it would happen—always shrugged it off as media talk. That night at dinner Tony and his Army mate sat and talked about how exciting it would be to go and how they hoped they would be called up.

I sat there stunned—wondering how he could say that in front of me, with no idea of how it might affect me if he went to war. That was the moment I realized I wasn't even a minor priority to Tony. That moment, I made up my mind. I was going to end it that night. I could no longer keep being the perfect girlfriend, just waiting for him to realize it.

We went back to his place in silence. We sat down in the den as I wondered how to say what I knew I had to tell him. Tony turned on the television—to avoid talking to me, I thought.

Then we heard the news flash. Suddenly it was true—Tony was going to war. I instantly forgot about my decision to break up with him and cried my heart out. Tony sat stunned. The phone started ringing, and he spoke to his buddies about it—full of excitement. But when he spoke to me, there was a strange sadness in his voice.

Neither of us knew what to say or do over the next week while he prepared to go. Six months, they said he would be gone—maybe longer. And nobody knew what to expect; they said on the news that everyone had to prepare for the worst, because war is always dangerous.

I spent the week in a fog. I went through the motions with Tony. We hugged, we kissed, we promised to write, and he left for the airport before I had time to make any sense of it.

The only thing I was thinking as he left was that I had to do all I could to support him. I cried for so many hours that night my throat ached from the sobbing. Then I told myself that what I had to do was to make his time away easier.

I wrote to him every day—filling my letters with cheery thoughts. Telling him tiny details and stories of my life. Writing him funny poems to keep his spirits up. Reminding him of some of our happier times together.

After a month, I started getting letters back from him. This was our new life for the next six months. Every night, I just sat down and wrote everything that was in my head and my heart. I thought about nothing except making his time easier. I wasn't concentrating on being the perfect girlfriend anymore. I was concentrating on doing what was best for Tony—truly loving him for the first time, without expecting or wanting anything in return.

He came back after six long months and it felt like we were see-ing each other for the first time. He produced a dazzling diamond ring that night and asked me to be his wife. I accepted, and over the next few weeks he explained to me how he had seen so much of my personality in those letters—how those letters had captured something he didn't even know I had.

I realized then that in all my efforts to be the perfect girlfriend, I had kept Tony from seeing the real me. I realized he wasn't looking for perfection; he was just looking for a real person. Tony doesn't love me because I do everything right; he loves me in spite of my faults. I think he even loves me *because* of my faults.

All I had to do was let go of the fears I held about him seeing that I was not perfect and allow him to see me for who I really was.

I know now how close we came to the end. If Tony had never gone to war, we would have broken up that night without ever real-ly knowing each other.

That war gave us the chance to know each other, and I will be forever grateful. How tragic it would have been to be so near to my soul mate for so long without ever realizing it.

Thanks to our time apart and those letters, we each discovered the real me lurking behind the "perfect girlfriend." And we might just live happily ever after.

—Shelley Wake

Sometimes our belief in who we need to be gets in the way of who we really are. We hide our own radiance from the world with an artificial version of ourselves that we think everyone else wants. How wrong we are. Real relationships aren't based on the pretense of perfection. True intimacy is the coming together of two people who trust each other enough to be their genuine selves. It is only when we let down our guard and let go of that fake barrier that the perfect love that exists within all of us can emerge.

Generations

WHO UNDERSTANDS MUCH, FORGIVES MUCH.

—*MADAME DE STAËL*

I AM A DAUGHTER. I am in kindergarten. My grandmother is asleep on the couch, wrapped in the crocheted coverlet that is her cocoon. She is always resting on the couch, except when she sits up to tell us to wear our sweaters on hot summer days.

My grandmother was once vibrant and beautiful—an artist and French teacher who studied one summer at the Sorbonne. At the age of forty, she married my grandfather, a charming Irishman, and soon gave birth to my mother.

Then, three years later, when she was giving birth to my uncle, something went wrong. She developed a problem with her pituitary artery, causing adrenal deficiencies and hypothyroidism. From that point on, she was sluggish and spent most days in bed. When my mother was three, her childhood was over; she found herself responsible for her little brother and often for her mother as well.

Now my grandmother lives with us. My mother is always mad at her for complaining about her sore feet and refusing to go shopping for new shoes. My grandmother says her feet hurt too much to go out. My mother thinks she is exaggerating the pain and keeps bringing home new black-laced shoes for my grandmother to try on. None are good enough.

I am a daughter taking on the role of mother. I am fourteen. I am sitting by the living room window on a stormy night; it is three in the morning, and I am waiting for my parents to come home. They have been at a party, and I know they have been drinking heavily. Every time a car passes by, I startle. I don't know how to make sense of the mix of fear and rage that I feel. If they die, will I be left to raise my younger brother and sisters?

This is such a change from my earlier childhood, when my

mother and father took such good care of us. I remember Mom taking us to the park or hiding our lunches for treasure hunts, and Dad playing football with all the neighborhood kids.

Things are so different now, as my mother and father struggle with depression and alcoholism. As the oldest child, I feel a great weight of responsibility. I hate being the bad mother, the one who yells at them when I discover that they've been drinking. When I come home after school and find my mother passed out on the bed, or when my dad calls and says he won't be home until very late, I get so angry. But mostly I'm scared, and I don't understand.

I am a mother. I am twenty-five. As I bring my firstborn son home from the hospital, I realize that the Lamaze classes prepared me for birth, but not for life after birth. Carrying him out of the hospital, I cannot believe they're going to let me take him home. I don't know what I'm doing. When is the real mom going to show up?

When I nurse him, the pain is excruciating. No one told me about this. Determined to nurse, I sit and cry, my nipples bleeding and my uterus cramping. I lock myself in my room with him, crying, nursing, and rocking. I am in love with him, and I am more exhausted than I ever thought possible. I want a mother.

In the midst of my deepest joy, I begin to grieve. More than any other time in my life, I want a mother who can come and tell me about all this, who can teach me how to be a mother myself, who can reassure me that I'm doing a good job.

But my mother is still in the difficult years. She and my father are still struggling with depression and still drinking. They're on the verge of separating and have little energy for anything else but their own problems, so my mother is not here.

I grow and I learn, and I discover, day by day, that I am the real mom.

I am a mother. I am a daughter. I am forty-five. I never thought that I would be the one to get a divorce, but life doesn't always turn out the way you plan. For eleven years my ex-husband and I have shared custody of our three sons. I have learned much about myself in this process and have also worked hard to calm any of the boys' fears that they might be abandoned. Now I am happily remarried, my sons are young men, and my youngest child—my daughter—is in kindergarten.

I am on my way to see my mother and to help her organize her apartment.

My mother's body is falling apart. Heart problems, breast cancer, and osteoporosis have all taken their toll. The bones in her right foot are deteriorating, and her hipbones are so thin that the doctors cannot take any bone from them to rebuild her foot. She complains about the pain and is always searching for shoes that will help.

I pick up a box stuffed with receipts, dollar bills, medicine bottles, and old photos, and ask her where I should begin. She looks at me, her eyes filling up with tears.

"I'm so overwhelmed." Her voice breaks. "I remember going through my mother's things and throwing away so much against her will." Now she is sobbing.

"I have so much guilt about my mother," she stammers. I have a hard time making out her words because she is crying so hard. "I was so mean to her about her shoes. I didn't understand."

My heart opens, and for the first time in a long while I feel no need to defend against her. I put down the box and go over to her, putting my arms around her shrinking body. She feels so fragile and vulnerable. I clasp her head against my shoulder. "It's okay, Mom. It's all okay."

I give her a long hug. My mother and I have both suffered, we've both made mistakes, but we've both loved, too. I remember that we are all making it up as we go along, doing the best we can with whatever we've got.

In that moment, I understand. I am grateful to be standing here with her, both of us tearful, holding each other tight—aware of a grace that has always been with us, weaving through it all.

—Denise Roy

"Generations," adapted from the essay by the same name in *My Monastery Is a Minivan: Where the Daily Is Divine and the Routine Becomes Prayer.*

None of us is perfect. Whether our childhoods were happy, miserable, or somewhere in between, most of us wish our parents could have been different in some way. Almost always, they were doing the best they knew how to do at the time. If we look back to our parents' childhoods and at their entire lives, we begin to understand how they became the people they are. When we understand, we can forgive. When we let go of regrets and expectations about what our parents (or siblings, or children) should be and accept them for who they are, we find that all-powerful, omnipresent grace.

Sacred Sand Painting

WE SPEND OUR LIVES DOING THINGS WE HATE,
TO BUY THINGS WE DON'T NEED AND IMPRESS PEOPLE
WE DON'T LIKE.
—ANONYMOUS

IF THERE IS ONE THING that imprisons us in misery and keeps us from happiness and our Divine path in life, it is our ego. We think we are our ego. We nurture and protect our ego and think that it's the driver that will take us to success. Our ego is a driver, but it's a stunt driver, like in those races where the cars go around and around but never get anywhere—all for the amusement of the crowds in the stands that are gone the next day. That's the ego's idea of driving—make us go as fast as we can in circles.

To let go of our ego is to live authentically, as our real selves, not as everyone else expects us to be. When we let go of our ego we radiate pure light. We are magnets for others, not because we regale them with stories or accomplishments, but because of the natural confidence and love that emanates from us. The kind of a person who consistently releases his ego is extremely rare, but when you meet him or her, it is an extraordinary experience.

I met one such person several years ago, and I will never forget him. Matthew was a poet and artist who gave workshops at a resort in the desert. Everyone told me that the Sacred Art of Sand Painting demonstration was an absolute must. My schedule was full, and sand painting sounded boring to me, but everyone was so adamant about the workshop that I figured I'd better go—just to make sure I wasn't missing anything.

Matthew was an unassuming man, of average height and build, scruffily attractive, dressed in old jeans, sporting auburn-brown facial hair—nothing too remarkable. But as soon as he began to speak, everyone in the room was under his spell. He charmed us with tales of the desert, poetry he'd written, and music he played on an old American Indian instrument called a Lakota six-hole flute. But, the amazing thing was that as he talked, he created the most incredible sand painting on the floor. His audience gasped, taking in the beauty and the wonder of the intricate piece of art he gingerly drew with the colorful minerals of the Earth. We all wanted to keep it, shellac it, preserve it, take it home, and hang it in our living rooms. I'm sure that he could have sold that painting for hundreds, maybe thousands of dollars to any one of several people in that room. But that was not to be. As our time together came to an end, Matthew simply took a long stick and blended the sand together, dismantling his extraordinary artwork.

I was astonished at the humility of that simple action. It struck me instantly that he didn't need lasting physical evidence of his talent; he didn't need to keep it around to be applauded and fussed over in order to feed his ego. He wasn't afraid of the loss or anxious about proving himself. He knew that everything he needed he had inside of himself, and he had the faith that he could always draw on his talent.

Before I left the resort, I bought a little sand painting in a small glass terrarium to keep as a reminder to myself to forget my ego and my need to create grand achievements, and to remember to do things for the sheer joy of the present moment.

—Kathy Cordova

It has been said that the journey is the reward. How often do we forget this simple truth? When we experience the joy of the process—in work, relationships, or creative endeavors—we let go of anxiety, fear, and stress. And we set our passion free.

Facing the Scorpions

NOTHING IN LIFE IS TO BE FEARED. IT IS ONLY TO BE UNDER-
STOOD.

—*MARIE CURIE*

I WAS LOOKING for something when I came to America at age
nineteen; I just didn't know what. As one of six children, I wanted
to do something on my own, to have an adventure before attend-
ing the university, as my father insisted we all do. As an au pair, I
worked for a kind couple in a university town, so I could take classes when I'd saved enough money. The world would show me what
I was looking for, of that I was confident.

I met him two weeks after I arrived. At a party given by another
au pair, he exuded confidence and self-assurance. I was entranced
by his intelligence and ambition; he was a student at the university
and knew exactly what he wanted to do with his life. He courted me
with the same intensity that drove the rest of his life, and I was
drawn into a whirlwind of intoxication. Never before had I felt so
needed. He wanted to spend all his time with me, and somehow I
felt I'd found my purpose. After five heady weeks he proposed
marriage and I accepted.

Rapidly, however, the intensity and passion that marked our
courtship shifted into control and manipulation. At first he seemed
to support my dreams; he insisted I finish both undergraduate and
graduate degrees. After awhile I realized what he really wanted was
for me to have a high-paying job. Money was all-important to him;
he controlled every penny and how it was spent. One day I came
home from work to find a brand-new, flashy sports car in our drive-
way. When I asked him about it he announced he had bought it for
himself, declaring without a hint of irony, "I bought it with *your*
bonus!" This control extended to every aspect of our lives—from
where we went to dinner to where we spent our vacations. If I

tried to express my opinion, he'd ignore it, or worse, put me down.

Developing friendships was difficult, because he didn't want me to have any interests besides him. He expected me to spend all my free time at home. Although I had friends at work, I was afraid to tell him. I knew it would cause him to become verbally abusive and jealous. Still, I figured his behavior revealed how much he needed me. His childhood had been lousy; his parents neglected him. If I just loved him enough, I believed he would be okay and would feel secure enough to change. I would go out of my way to please him, to avoid upsetting him . . . as if it were my fault he treated me the way he did. Never before had I felt so unsure of myself; my self-esteem was completely based on whether or not I could please him. At that, I was a failure.

As the years passed, we had two beautiful children, and his career took off. He wouldn't help me with the kids, once remarking, "The kids would have to be on their deathbeds before I would get up at night for them." He never gave them baths or put them to bed, and he refused to read to them, saying only, "My parents never read to me."

As his job success grew, so did his moodiness. Although he never physically abused us, he would throw things against the wall in fits of fury. I would find myself trying to stay ten steps ahead of him, to read his mood by the way he got out of the car in the evening. My life embodied the phrase, "walking on eggshells."

He began working later and later. Some nights he didn't come home at all. He would tell me he was at planning meetings for his new company. One night, however, I stopped by his office. Hoping to appease him, I brought him some dinner. I found him intimately involved with his secretary. He blamed me for the affair, saying that I had driven him to it. Although I was angry, I maintained a cool composure. Even in that situation I didn't want to upset him further. Because of the children, I wasn't ready to dissolve the marriage, and he promised me he would never see her again. I believed him when he told me he didn't want to hurt the family, that he would do anything to keep us together. My hope was that we could have a new beginning.

I tried to move forward, but it soon became apparent that he had not changed. He called me from work one day to ask if his girl-friend had called. She was angry with him and threatened to contact me. I realized I had been the fool again. Fear seized me; as horribly humiliating as life was with him, a life without him was incomprehensible. What would our friends think? What about the kids? The house? We owned so much together, had built an incredible, affluent lifestyle. Without him I would have nothing. I clung to these external aspects of our life, as if they were a frame that would hold us together. But the frame was our relationship, not those things, and it was crumbling. I hated myself and the lie I was living.

I packed up the kids in the Chevy Suburban and went to live with his sister in another state. He begged us to come home, made countless promises. After six months I broke down and believed him . . . again. Then I went back to the most gruesome period of my life. I soon discovered he was still seeing the other woman. I would come home from work and find her thong underpants in my bed, her blond hair on my pillow. They were flagrant and unabashed, throwing their affair in my face every chance they got. One day when I was at the grocery store picking up film from my camera, I opened the package to find a roll of pictures of the two of them in Hawaii. Tears blinded me as I finally realized my marriage was a joke and I was nothing but an object of ridicule.

I took the kids, moved in with a girlfriend, and filed for divorce. The proceedings were ugly, vicious, and expensive. His influence over me was far-reaching. He made horrible threats . . . threats that tormented me on many sleepless nights. He'd vow I wouldn't get custody of the kids; I wouldn't get a penny of his money. Panic penetrated every inch of me. I was deeply afraid of him and what my life would be like. I had never been alone before and had grown accustomed to a very comfortable way of life. I knew I needed help; that I couldn't get through this alone.

At just the right moment, a dear friend invited me on an experi-ence that changed my life. She had seen a flyer for Vision Quest, a spiritual transformation adventure, and wanted me to go with her.

The adventure consisted of spending a week in the Arizona desert, three days of which we would spend completely alone fasting. This was an enormous leap for me, as I was terrified of scorpions and snakes and had never camped a day or missed a meal in my life. But I was desperate and willing to try anything. The orientation inspired me as I listened to twelve other women share their personal transitions and their courage to face their fears. Nonetheless, I set out that first day by myself with trepidation. I was grateful that we were given rituals and meditations, which I mechanically performed to keep my mind off all that could happen to me out there.

Then, after many hours of this, I saw a scorpion. Scuttling toward me, it was quick and ominous. I wanted to run and find someone to help. But then I realized how ridiculous I would appear. So I simply stopped. As a child would poke a creature with a stick, so did I observe and examine it. Something inside me let go, and I experienced joy as my fear turned to amazement at this small wonder of creation.

I realized that my fears were like that scorpion; many were hidden inside the dark caverns of my mind. Only by watching them move on the desert floor would I overcome their power over me. So I dug deep and pulled them out. I took every threat and insult my husband had poisoned me with and examined the way it controlled me. He said I wouldn't get a penny. Once I squarely looked this threat in its beady black eye, I realized what a wonderful support group I had in my parents and friends; I would manage. He said I wouldn't get to see the kids. I knew this was wildly improbable, but even if it were possible, I realized I would always have my deep love for them. He would never be able to touch the love and strength that I had within me. One by one, the venomous stings that I had endured over the years dissipated in that hot desert air.

The third night in the desert was brilliant, with the stars above me and the sense of freedom within me. I had done it. I'd found my place of power in the center of my soul; I was ready to return to my life with a new sense of self and purpose. I had finally found my adventure in America, though it had nothing to do with where

I was or who I met. What I'd been looking for at nineteen, and found twenty-six years later, was the sense of freedom that comes from knowing I was worthy of love and I was loved—by God, myself, and my family and friends. I learned that the adventure is the journey we all take within ourselves and traverse throughout our lifetime. We move a little farther down the road as we dig out the scorpions, study them, and set them free.

—Dominique's story, written by Amy Moellering

Our fears are merely illusions created by our egos to keep us trapped in the dark crevices of our misery. Once we shine the light on our fears, we see them for what they truly are—nothing but apparitions haunting our minds. When exposed to the light of love, they vanish.

The Lesson of the Leaf

AS YOU RELEASE, SO WILL YOU BE RELEASED.

—A COURSE IN MIRACLES

SOME YEARS AGO I was spending a month primarily by myself on a retreat in Australia. I was immersed in nature; I didn't read, listen to television, or talk on the telephone. I had no communication with my wife or friends. My communication was only with God.

One day I was walking by a stream and decided to sit on a large rock that looked over the stream. After about twenty minutes I happened to look up at a branch of a nearby tree to see a leaf fall from it.

The wind took hold of the leaf and blew it in a gentle circle. To my utter surprise, it landed right next to me on the rock. Immediately I felt that there was some kind of special message to be given to me by my new friend, the leaf. I focused all my attention on the leaf, beseeching it to reveal its meaning.

A few minutes later the wind came up and took the leaf high above my head. Slowly it landed in the stream and floated gently away until it disappeared.

I learned a lesson from the leaf that day. When you have total trust and faith in God, you can let go of whatever you are holding onto that makes you feel secure. I learned not to be fearful but to flow gently with the wind and the stream of life.

For me it was a powerful lesson of surrendering to God, surrendering to love, and letting go of the things that I was holding to that kept me separate from God.

There are no words to describe the joy and bliss that I felt that day. Later I came across a beautiful waterfall. I jumped into the pool below, feeling the cold water cascade over my head. It felt like God was blessing me—baptizing me into a new life of freedom,

trust, and faith. I felt the sacredness of that moment when I surrendered myself to God and love.

—Jerry Jampolsky, M.D.

The things of the world that we cling to so tightly—money, pres-
tige, the need to be the best—often keep us separate from God and
other people. When we release our attachment to those things that
we are most afraid of losing, we find the freedom to flow with life as
God intends—gently, peacefully, like a leaf on an autumn day.

Freeing the Wild Woman Within

LEAP AND THE NET WILL APPEAR.

—*JULIE CAMERON*

I FELT LIKE A TRAPPED WILD ANIMAL. I hated my job as a research analyst. The work was dull and uninspiring, nothing more than glorified word processing. Even more punishing than the work was the micromanagement style of my boss. Her misguided comments cut into me like fangs, criss-crossing my soul with lacerations—wounds that never quite healed on the weekends.

I dreamed of quitting, but rent, credit card balances, and car payments held me back. And besides, I'd never been able to muster enough confidence to go after what I really wanted in life. I'd always been taught it was more important to fit in and not make waves. I was so averse to conflict that I once even changed my college major just to avoid a confrontation with a guy in class who was harassing me. Single and without any other means of support, my choices were to stay and suffer, or to search and find another research position.

So I scoured the Help Wanted sections, networked with former colleagues, and contacted placement agencies, drumming up enough interviews to give me hope of a quick exit. Unfortunately, none of the interviews panned out. Then I saw a promising ad for a research analyst at a health insurance company.

During the first interview, I met with two project managers and several research analysts. Everyone seemed pleasant, but the work sounded tedious and I slipped into ambivalence halfway through the interview.

When I got home I started to panic. I knew I had delivered a mediocre performance, and I began to fear that I'd ruined yet another opportunity. I quickly wrote a thank you note, forcing myself to fill it with energetic statements and praise for the company. Amazingly, a project manager called a few days later to ask me to return for a second interview with the director.

The interview with the director was going fine until she relayed to me that her project manager was surprised to receive my upbeat thank you note because he thought I was uninterested in the job. Then, during one of those pivotal life moments, she asked me why I wanted this job.

At that moment I felt my rational mind melting into my heart. Against all the interviewing advice I'd ever received, I told her the truth: My boss didn't appreciate me, my job was dull, my spirit was crushed, and my work environment was oppressive. The release of all the feelings I'd been trying to hide was like a dam breaking. I burst into tears.

She handed me some tissues and pointed me toward the ladies' room, where I sat in a stall and cried for half an hour. Every time I attempted to gather my composure, it spattered all over the linoleum again.

Finally, my tears dried up long enough for me to go back into her office, retrieve my coat, apologize, and thank her for the interview. Once in the car, though, the torrent of tears came rushing back. By the time I got home, I knew that I was not crying out of sadness but out of relief.

I didn't want that research job or any other research job. I realized I had never wanted to be a researcher. I stumbled into that field by default because I never had the courage to find out what I really wanted to do with my life.

Then I made my first proactive decision. I decided, for the first time in my life, to let go of my fear and follow my heart. I wrote the director a thank you note and explained my breakdown as the realization that taking this research job would be a mistake. I told her that I was determined to find my own path and follow it, wherever it took me.

The following day, I told an older, wiser colleague about the experience I'd had at the insurance company. She suggested I read *Women Who Run with the Wolves* by Clarissa Pinkola Estés. It was love at first read. With each turn of the page, my spiritual wounds healed a little bit more. When I finished the book, I couldn't stop telling other women about its inspiring message. I felt energized, and I wanted the world to know I had a wild woman inside me clawing to get out and live the life she deserved to be living. A new-found power coursed through my veins.

Soon I found myself meeting spiritually gifted people at every turn in the road—including my future husband, who probably never would have been attracted to the old, repressed me. I connected with a caring career counselor who helped me recognize my need to be doing something creative for a living. During a noontime stroll, a concerned colleague told me that quitting one job without having another job was one of the most liberating things he had ever done and encouraged me to do the same. That day I took the biggest chance of my life—I took a chance on myself and quit!

Quitting a job without the safety net of another frightened me, but for the first time in many years I felt alive. I signed up with a temporary agency to do presentation graphics and had steady work for all but two weeks of the following year. With each new job assignment, I expanded my design skills and portfolio.

But the most amazing part of my experience was that at every job I met women who confided to me that they, too, disliked their jobs and wanted to make a career change, but didn't have the self-confidence to do it. Their stories validated my decision to follow the call of the wild.

One year later, I was contacted by a new agency for a marketing communications position at a high tech company. I knew instantly that the man who interviewed me was the compassionate, inspiring boss I'd always wanted. By the time I got back to work, he had already contacted the agency saying he wanted to hire me!

It's been six years, and I'm still working for this marvelous man, doing great, creative work in a job I love. Ironically, a good friend and researcher got a job several years ago at that same health insurance company I'd interviewed with, working for the same director who interviewed me that frigid, December day. When I asked my friend recently about the director, he told me that she had left her position to make a career change—to do something she had always wanted to do.

I may never know if my letter had any impact on her decision to move on to something more fulfilling. But I do know that the quality and breadth of our lives improves immeasurably when, as women, we believe in ourselves and let go of our fears enough to free the wild woman within.

—Julianne Nardone

Fear imprisons us more than walls of stone. Too often, we let fear hold us back from experiencing our greatest potential. We're afraid of what people will think, that we're not smart or talented enough, or that our dreams are too big. What glorious lives are in store for us when we let go of our fear and leap?

Release of Revenge

IT WILL BE GIVEN YOU TO SEE YOUR BROTHER'S WORTH WHEN
ALL YOU WANT FOR HIM IS PEACE. AND WHAT YOU WANT FOR
HIM YOU WILL RECEIVE.
—A COURSE IN MIRACLES

"HERPES?" I asked in disbelief.

"Genital herpes," confirmed the doctor.

I burst into tears. The pain I'd been experiencing over the last two days was excruciating—like nothing I'd ever felt before. I'd heard that urinary tract infections hurt like that and just assumed that's what I had. I had no clue that the intense burning I was feeling was not just a common ailment, but an incurable venereal disease.

While my body pulsed with pain, my mind raced with shame, fear, and remorse.

My life was ruined. Now, I thought, I'll never get married, never have kids, and never have any kind of a normal relationship again. I'd be branded with the scarlet letter H forever. And to add insult to injury, the guy that infected me had just unceremoniously dumped me.

Jack had looked great on paper. Tall, handsome, successful, he owned a house on top of a hill with a view of the ocean. His picture fit perfectly in the frame I'd constructed of the kind of a man I should marry.

For months we had a wonderful time, or so I fooled myself into thinking. The eventual dumping was one of those baffling cases that women hate most, where the last time you saw each other, everything seemed fine, then you don't hear from the guy for two weeks.

I had left for a business trip and he told me he'd call, but he didn't. When I returned, still no call. I called him and left a message—he didn't call back. I went over and over our last date, trying to figure what I could have said or done to make our relationship self-destruct so seamlessly. I retraced every word, every action, dissecting and analyzing everything, but I came up with no answer.

Swallowing any shred of dignity that I might have had left, I called until he answered the phone in person and prodded him into finally saying that he didn't think the relationship was working. No concrete reason. It just didn't *feel* right anymore.

I was devastated. Then I was angry. Really angry. I started to remember every time he'd been a jerk, which was a lot of times, and beat myself up for putting up with him for so long and then letting him dump me in the end.

And now I discovered he'd left me a little going away present that, unlike him, would be around until death do us part.

I couldn't believe I'd been so stupid. I couldn't believe he'd been so rotten. My disbelief turned to hatred. I can't remember ever really hating anyone before, but I hated him with all the intensity of my physical and emotional pain.

My days and nights were consumed with thoughts of revenge. I refused to victimize myself again by calling and confronting him— I knew it wouldn't do any good. What would he do? Say he was sorry and hang up, or, worse, just hang up.

Yet I knew I would not rest until vengeance was mine.

I decided I was done with men for a while. I threw away that old picture frame and started anew.

Two months later, I met my future husband.

He, too, was tall, handsome, and successful, but also equally infatuated with me and, thankfully, understanding about my condition. We fell in love.

I should have been happy, but there was still a dark place in my heart. Despite my joy in my new relationship, I still seethed with anger toward Jack.

We lived in a small town, but strangely, I had not seen him since we broke up. Still, I knew it was just a matter of time until I would run into him. I imagined the scenario in great detail—me strolling up to him, introducing my new boyfriend, and rubbing it in his face about how happy we were together. Of course when this happened, I would be looking fabulous. He would kick himself for having let me go and live forever in regret, or so played the scene in my head.

Days and weeks passed, but still there was no sign of him. I frequented places I knew he hung out, so that I could maneuver our "chance" meeting. I could not get this jerk out of my mind, and wherever we went, I was always looking out of the corner of my eye for my opportunity for revenge.

I was crazy and obsessed. At the time, I was reading a book in which something similar happened to the author. She tells the story of being stood up by a boyfriend and how angry she was. Unconditional forgiveness felt too much like being a victim, but she didn't know how to do the spiritually right thing without being a doormat. So she surrendered the situation to God and asked for a miracle. Then she repeated a prayer to herself, forgiving the guy, and wishing him the peace of God.

I decided to give it a try, so, I prayed and asked God to release me from this all-encompassing anger. Then I repeated my own prayer, "I forgive you Jack, and wish you the peace of God," over and over and over again. I was surprised to find myself gradually growing more at peace. The revenge thoughts began to fade.

Just as I was beginning to feel at peace, it happened. My boyfriend and I were going out to dinner. It was a nice restaurant and we were all dressed up—looking great. We made our way through the crowded bar area, my boyfriend a few steps ahead of me.

And there, sitting on a bar stool all by himself, was the object of my vengeful fantasies. Jack caught my eye immediately, looked me over appreciatively from head to toe and said, "I hear through the grapevine that you're in love."

The moment I had dreamed of so many times! A perfect setup. Now, just to get my boyfriend back over here, introduce him, and rhapsodize about how wonderful he was and how happy we were together.

But something stopped me. I didn't follow through with the

plan I'd fantasized about so many times. In that moment I realized, to my surprise, that I had let go of my anger.

Instead of hatred, I just felt warmth and friendliness toward Jack. Thoughts of rage and revenge were completely gone.

I just smiled serenely and responded, "Yes, I am in love. Good to see you," and I meant it, as I walked away from my past and toward my future.

—Michelle Steele

We've all heard that revenge is sweet, but isn't forgiveness much sweeter? Revenge lasts but a moment, but forgiveness lingers in our hearts—a golden glow that warms us even in the coldest times. We remember that we are all one—whatever we give, we receive. When we give love, compassion, forgiveness, and peace, they always return to us.

A Tree Grows in the Desert

TO BE IS TO LIVE WITH GOD.

—*RALPH WALDO EMERSON*

WE HAD ONLY LIVED in Washington state for a year or two, and I was still getting my bearings and acclimating myself to the differences from Connecticut, which had been my lifelong home. I was especially homesick for New England in autumn, when I knew all the maples, oaks, and elms in Connecticut would be afire with scarlet, blazing orange, and shimmering deep-yellow leaves. The sky would be blue; the air crisp and pure, and fallen leaves would crackle and crunch cheerfully underfoot. Here in the Northwest, leaves make a feeble attempt at turning pale yellow before succumbing to brown.

After four moves with three small children during our first year in the Northwest, we had finally settled in a place that was beginning to feel like home. The small town in a valley below the foothills of the Cascade Mountains had much of the charm of rural New England, and we had found a house we loved. Clinching the decision was the fact that there was a lovely old church of our denomination in town.

One of the women from our new congregation invited me to join a small group that was traveling to central Oregon in November for a regional women's retreat. I was still feeling a bit lonely and out of my element, and a retreat seemed to be just what I needed.

Our retreat was east of the Cascade Mountains in an area of the Pacific Northwest that is desert, with barren, brown, and windswept hills that are drenched in 360 days of sunshine per year. The theme of our weekend retreat was "Springs in the Desert," which seemed a portentous blessing to me. Despite the heavy outward rains at home, my inner landscape felt parched and barren. One of the ways that I had tried to get to know people and to make myself feel more at home in our new community was through volunteer and committee work, especially within my church. I had taken on several roles and jobs, particularly with children, my passion. But the tasks had quickly become so time- and energy-consuming that going to church felt like work, not respite and worship. I felt like I had taken on too much, and I was overwhelmed with all the responsibilities I felt to my church and my family, although I felt that if I didn't do all these things, they wouldn't get done.

On a quiet afternoon at the retreat, I went outside to relax and write in the sunshine. A good sitting-rock on a hillside overlooked the valley of waving golden grasses, dotted with boulders here and there. There were hardly any trees, and the few that grew there were short and scrubby, sturdily hunkered close to the ground to survive the incessant winds.

Perched on the warm rock, I anchored my paper with small pebbles against the breeze. A gnarled little brush of a tree stood close by, no taller than I, its branches twisted from years of defense against the gale. It seemed to cling precariously to the rocky, sandy hillside, with nothing beyond sheer will holding it in place. I thought of the tall, graceful evergreens swaying behind my house in Washington; and also remembered the beautiful, blazing autumn woods I was missing in Connecticut.

I tried to be at peace, but nagging thoughts of all the pressing things I needed to do once I got home were nipping at the edges of my brain. It seemed sometimes that the more I did, the more things there were that someone else expected me to do. My wise pastor, while appreciating the volunteering I did at church, was also aware of the stress my level of "busy-ness" added to my life. He had commented to me that perhaps I was too much of a "human doing" and not enough "human being." I found it very hard to just "be"—to be still and know that I am God.

I looked quizzically at the little tree. I don't think I spoke aloud; but I'll never be entirely certain. "Strange little tree," I thought (or said). "What good are you really? Too small to be of much consequence. Why aren't you tall and majestic like the stately Douglas Firs swaying in the breeze behind my house?"

And the tree answered, gently, "That's not my task."

"Why, then," I asked, "do you bear no fruit, like the laden apple, pear, and plum trees in the orchard valleys nearby, which feed and sustain so many?"

Again, "That's not my task."

"You don't even have beautiful leaves, like the maple trees of New England, to gladden the eye and give glory to God!"

"That's not my task," as gentle as before.

"You really aren't even big enough to give shade in this barren place!" I accused.

"It is not my task."

Somehow, the attitude of calm and purpose emanating from the little tree irritated me. Perhaps I was hearing in my own reproach all of the "shoulds" that I told myself I had to do—and didn't know how to say, "That task is not for me."

"Well, then—what *is* your task? Why are you here?"

"I am helping to hold this part of this hill in place. My roots strengthen the soil's grip on the hillside, so the grass has this place to grow. This is my task."

It was so simple. So clear. So self-assured. There was no expression of doubt, no "What if I can't hold enough of the hill in place?" There was no fretting about who was holding the next hill over in its place, no worrying that perhaps the roots should be extended to cover more ground. Not even any apology or remorse for not being all those other things that other trees are—shady, fruitful, colorful, or tall and regal.

At that moment, in that desert place, I felt the gushing of a new spring breaking through the dry earth of my anxiety. I understood that my creator was teaching me to *just be.* I realized with newfound clarity that I would never be able to hold down all the hillsides in the world; but most important, I realized that I didn't need to—it was not required of me to do it all; not everything was meant to be my task. I have my own small part of the hill to hold, and it is enough.

Even in the desert, when the time is right, flowers simply bloom where they are sown. There is living water flowing even in the parched land, and when I let myself *just be* beside the water, there I can flourish too.

—Barbara S. Greenstreet

We often think our value lies in what we do—the more and grander things we do, the better. We run around crazed; we think our busyness proves how important, how irreplaceable we are. Have you ever heard the expression, "God may use you, but he doesn't need you?" When we let go of all of our notions of what we should be doing and realize that we are worthwhile just as we are, we can relax. Our energy is not wasted frantically striving. Instead it is focused—inspired by joy and purpose.

Giving Up the Mask

YOU WOULDN'T WORRY SO MUCH WHAT EVERYBODY
THOUGHT OF YOU IF YOU KNEW HOW SELDOM THEY DID.
—*DR. PHIL MCGRAW*

NEVER LEAVE THE HOUSE WITHOUT MAKEUP. This law is as deeply ingrained in my psyche as "Thou shalt not commit adultery" or "Wait thirty minutes after eating to go swimming." I've been tempted to break all of these rules at one time or another, but the makeup rule tempts me daily.

I'd love to be like those fresh-faced moms dropping their kids off at preschool. No makeup, wrinkled blue jean overalls, strands of gray in their hair. They've probably been at home doing meaningful things, like science projects with their kids, baking cupcakes from scratch, or writing the Great American Novel, while I'm wasting time covering up the dark circles under my eyes.

But, no matter how tedious, it's difficult to go out into the world without my customary mask of foundation, lipstick, and mascara. I've always been taught, "Appearances count," and I never believed I appeared quite right without a layer of some sort between me and the outside world.

Several years ago a psychic told me that I'd been a colicky baby. No big surprise there; I'd heard the stories from my mother many times: Dad holding my eyelids shut to get me to go to sleep; Mom rocking my bassinet with her foot to soothe me as she tried to cook dinner; me, red-faced, screaming bloody murder day and night. The scenes were well etched in my memory from years of re-telling.

But the big revelation was what the psychic told me next—something that I didn't know, or hadn't let myself know until that moment. He told me that early experience had given me the feeling that I was "too much" for other people, and that I had spent the rest of my life toning myself down a few notches so that I could fit in.

His words rang instantly true, although I'd never realized it until that moment. Always the smart kid in class, I learned to stop raising my hand to volunteer answers—it made the other kids resent me. My extravagant ideas were usually met with exasperation by my overworked mother. "That makes too much of a mess," she'd say about an art project or recipe I dreamed up. Any big ambitions I had were discounted or discouraged by family members grounded in their own limited realities. "Don't get your hopes up," they'd say, trying only to protect me from disappointment, but squashing a little bit of me every time.

Yet, there was an ironic flip side. At the same time I believed I was "too much," I also had a nagging feeling I was not enough. In other words, I always wanted to be exactly what I wasn't. I was brainy, but I wanted to be beautiful. I was a brunette, while I pined for blond hair. I was a bookworm, but I dreamed of being a cheerleader. We lived in a poor, run-down neighborhood, but I struggled to fit in with the kids from the other side of town with the big houses and the nice clothes.

So there you have my screwed up version of myself—trying to hold back my true self to be accepted, while desperately wanting to be everything I wasn't.

After college, when I moved 3,000 miles across the country where nobody knew me, I was free to reinvent myself in the image of my own fantasy. I shaped up at a trendy San Francisco gym, got Saks and Nordstrom credit cards, and even highlighted my hair. To Californians, my home state of Virginia was deep in the land of Dixie, and I was an exotic Southern Belle—not just a poor little bookworm from the wrong side of town.

When I first moved to California, I remember meeting a guy at a party and telling him that I was from Virginia. With thoughts of Thomas Jefferson and tobacco plantations in his head, he assumed out loud, "Oh, you must be from a very old, established family!" With a haughty, "Oh, yes," and a flip of my hair, my working-class heritage became only a hazy recollection. My mask was glued on tight.

The image I'd created looked good on the outside. I had a

glamorous-sounding job. I was making lots of money and had lots of dates. And, most important, I was succeeding in a conventional fashion—finally getting ardent approval from everyone—from my family in Virginia to my VP of sales.

By this time, I had unconsciously built my entire life around a cycle of proving myself—a sales career that demanded constant performance, a new boyfriend every couple of months, obsessively working out. Despite the obvious downsides (stress, lack of a lasting relationship, the struggle to maintain the image, to name a few), I stayed entrenched in my treadmill of achieving, being applauded and rewarded, and then forcing myself do it all over again.

Then, everything changed. I got married. I had a baby. I quit my job.

Suddenly, everything I had valued about myself was gone—my looks and well-toned body, my job and money, and, I believed, any kind of sex appeal I ever had. The mask crumbled. And in its place were piles of laundry, a demanding husband, a crying baby, and my old insecure self.

I would fall into bed exhausted and wake up in the middle of the night, filled with anxiety, unable to go back to sleep. I felt completely hopeless.

It is said that when the student is ready the teacher will appear.

My teacher materialized in the form of Sarah, an unconventional therapist who combined massage and intuitive counseling in her tiny living room. One day, feeling stressed and tired, I decided to treat myself to a massage. I found a discount coupon for a massage in the newspaper; I didn't find out about the therapy until I walked in the door. Sarah began massaging the soles of my feet and by the time she was up to my back she told me—as if she had known me my whole life, instead of just meeting me 30 minutes ago—"You are too hard on yourself. You need to be kinder to yourself." Those words hit me like a brick. I started sobbing mid-massage. It had never occurred to me to be kind to myself; I was too busy forcing my square self into a round hole. I started therapy with Sarah the next week.

Our sessions got to the point quickly. Every problem I *thought* I had—feeling fat, a thoughtless husband, a friend who hurt my feelings—weren't my real problems at all, but symptoms of one big whopper of a problem. Deep down I felt worthless. I was petrified the world would discover my secret, so I spent my whole life proving to the world—and myself—that I *was* pretty, skinny, successful—worthy.

Me, worthless?! I couldn't admit it at first. I had an ego to protect. I was scared. What if I *really* was worthless? Or, maybe worse, what if I decided I really *was* worthwhile, just by virtue of "existing"? If that were true, wouldn't I just end up lollygagging around, watching *Beverly Hills 90210* reruns, eating chocolate, and feeling content in my newfound worthiness? Without the fear, where would be the motivation? It had worked reasonably well up to now, hadn't it? Wasn't achievement how we measured worth? Wasn't that *healthy*?

I continued therapy, but I resisted the insights. I moved on, but not forward. I lost the weight. The colic disappeared and my daughter became delightful. I started a home-based business, and in a short time had some amazing success. Still, I was depressed. My insomnia was worse. Now that a light had been shone on my charade, I couldn't hide anymore—my mask felt transparent.

I had no choice but to quit resisting and completely surrender to my beliefs and fears about my self-worth. Digging deep down and acknowledging my fears helped them to melt away. When I could say, "Okay, I admit it. I'm worthless," I could see how ridiculous it sounded. Surrendering to those feelings somehow freed me. I no longer had to pretend I was something I wasn't. I realized that I'm a worthwhile human being by virtue of existing on this planet. I am a child of God—even if the house is a mess and I have cellulite on my thighs.

I know who I am—a loving—if indulgent—mother, a pretty good wife, someone who would rather read a book than run a marathon, and a lousy housekeeper, among a myriad of other traits that may or may not be valued by society, but are genuinely mine.

Still, old habits die hard, and the make-up thing is one small concession to my Southern Belle roots, my vanity, and the need for a little control over my blotchy skin.

But sometimes, when I wake up really early for a morning jog, I slip on my sunglasses, pull my hair into a ponytail, and run barefaced into the morning—without bothering to cover up those dark circles.

—Kathy Cordova

No one is too much or too little. We are all perfect—exactly as God created us.

CHAPTER 4

surrendering a problem

TROUBLE AND PERPLEXITY DRIVE US TO PRAYER, AND PRAYER
DRIVETH AWAY TROUBLE AND PERPLEXITY.
—*PHILLIP MELANCHTHON*

URRENDERING A PROBLEM is simply giving our troubles to God/a Higher Power/the Universe. Even though it's often a surrender of last resort, for most people it's the easiest type of surrender; it's got the most obvious upside. It's the kind of surrender that most of us have experienced sometime in our lives, especially when we were desperate.

After we've already done everything we can think of to figure out a solution, then we usually feel okay about giving it to God. After all, if we're out of options or we've bottomed out and we just don't have the will to fight any longer, what have we got to lose if we give the whole mess to God?

People in twelve-step programs know the awesome power of this type of surrender. The third step is "to turn our will and our lives over to the care of our Higher Power." The eleventh step is to seek "through prayer and meditation to improve our conscious contact with our Higher Power, praying only for knowledge of our Higher Power's will for us and the power to carry that out." Millions of people around the world have been released from their addictions by learning to Let Go and Let God.

The power in surrendering our problems to God comes from merely releasing the problem, not from asking for a specific solution. We need to just pray (or meditate, or whatever form of asking for help we choose), let go of the problem, continue to act, and listen for the answer—which may or may not be what we envision.

Martin Luther King, Jr., gives a wonderful example of this in his book *Strength to Love*. When Dr. King was leading the bus boycott in Montgomery, Alabama, they set up a carpool to help people get around. The carpool operated without problem for eleven months, but then, the mayor of Montgomery had had enough. He instructed the city's leading department to file proceedings making the carpool—or any other mode of transportation in support of the boycott—illegal. A hearing was set to decide the matter.

Dr. King writes how he dreaded telling supporters the news that the carpools would probably be closed down. This meant that they had only two choices: either they would all have to walk to work, or take the buses again and admit that the boycott had failed.

"When the evening (before the hearing) came," writes Dr. King, "I mustered sufficient courage to tell them the truth. I tried, however, to conclude on a note of hope. 'We have moved all of these months,' I said, 'in the daring faith that God is with us in our struggle. The many experiences of days gone by have vindicated that faith in a marvelous way. Tonight we must believe that *a way will be made out of no way.*'"

The next day, the hearing did not go well, and it looked like Dr. King and his supporters would lose, and the carpools would be outlawed. All seemed hopeless. Then, an amazing thing happened. At a brief recess, there was a commotion in the courtroom, and a reporter handed Dr. King the news, "The United States Supreme Court today unanimously ruled bus segregation unconstitutional in Montgomery, Alabama." Someone shouted from the back of the courtroom, "God Almighty has spoken from Washington!"

It's a good thing that Dr. King didn't pray to keep the carpool. God had a much better way of solving his problem!

In some cases, we may be resisting the inevitable. Giving the situation to God grants us peace, even in our sorrow. Mary, a friend of my mother's, tells one of the most moving stories of surrender I've ever heard. Many years ago, Mary, a new mother and just a child herself at seventeen, watched helplessly as her seven-month-old baby boy lie dying in the hospital with meningitis. She wept as she watched his tiny body stiffen and arch. His cries of pain were more than she could bear. "I prayed constantly," she says, "asking the Lord to heal him."

But the baby did not heal; he just got sicker. Finally Mary could not endure his suffering any longer, and she prayed a different prayer, releasing her son. "I prayed to the Lord to just take him. I surrendered him. Minutes later, he died. It was the hardest thing I've ever done, but I knew that's what I needed to do." Mary felt intense grief, and then, a sense of peace.

The experience has given the seventy-four-year-old great-grandmother and devout Christian a lesson she will always remember: "Every day is a surrender. If I could surrender my baby, then I can surrender anything." All of us will experience sorrow and grief in our lives. When physical healing doesn't come, we can give our pain to God and know that he will help heal our heart.

Michael J. Fox realized he needed to accept his diagnosis of Parkinson's disease, but he wasn't able to face it until the night he surrendered, as he describes in his book *Lucky Man*. One Christmas Eve, unhappy with himself and unable to sleep, he sat down in the middle of the night and began to write. He scribbled a litany of his problems, worries, and fears. When he couldn't write any longer, he said, "I looked over what I'd written, and wept. Whatever else this was, I realized, it was an instrument of surrender."

Up until that point, Michael had tried to deny a lot of his problems, including his diagnosis of Parkinson's disease. This surrender was a turning point, and the day after Christmas he called a therapist and began the work of facing his problems, including acceptance of his disease. He tells how he decided to take the journey that his health crisis led him to, instead of fighting it, and how he was "profoundly enriched" by the experience. He was able to let go of his resistance to his disease, acknowledge it, and clear the path to a fuller, much richer life than he ever had before. He renewed a love and trust with his wife, gained respect and admiration from millions of fans for his courage in facing his disease, and has been able to help legions of people with Parkinson's disease by raising awareness and lots of money through his foundation. We should all be so lucky to have such loving, supportive relationships and have such an impact on the world.

These stories illustrate the power of surrender when dealing with a tremendous problem that seems to have no good answer. In each case, surrender brought different kinds of miracles: A tangible, ground-breaking court decision in the case of Dr. King; peace and faith for Mary; or a change in perception and freedom for Michael J. Fox.

It's always inspiring to hear about how people have surrendered their greatest problems, but it's important to remember that any problem—no matter how large or small—can and should be surrendered.

An example of a minor problem I surrendered occurred when my son Carson was two and a half years old, and I thought I had the perfect plan. Several of the other moms in my neighborhood were all sending their kids to a local preschool three mornings a week. Life would be great! Carson could play with his friends, I could have some time to myself and even carpool with the other moms.

But like many plans, this one was not to be. On the first day of class, the preschool was a confused mob scene. The teachers didn't introduce themselves, and the whole atmosphere seemed cold and indifferent—not loving and safe like I had imagined. Most of the parents left right away, but I stuck around with the kids as we sat in a big circle for 45 minutes while the teacher explained the rules of the school in excruciating detail to a bunch of restless toddlers.

A few kids were off by themselves, crying hysterically, as harried aides sporadically offered a tissue or glass of water, but little real comfort. Carson clung to me and begged me not to leave. Despite all the wonderful things I'd heard about this school from friends, I had a strong gut feeling that this was not the right place for my son, and I have learned, especially when something affects my kids, to trust my gut. So we walked out, forfeited our deposit, and never returned.

My search for another preschool yielded nothing. The few that I liked had filled up months before, and the ones that had openings, I didn't like. Also, Carson, who had been so excited about the prospect of going to school, was suddenly resisting the idea. I considered keeping him home and forgetting about preschool entirely, but I knew that if I could find the right program he'd enjoy it, and I was really looking forward to that little bit of time to myself each week.

I called every preschool in the phone book and searched my brain for a solution. I prayed and asked for help, although I couldn't imagine what form it would take.

Amy, Carson's baby-sitter since he was four months old, had just left town to go away to college. Since we had no family nearby, Amy had evolved into almost a second mother to our children, and we all really missed her. I knew Amy used to teach at a local preschool that had a good reputation. Although the classes were full, I thought she might have some ideas for me, so I called her.

I was surprised to find her not away at college as I expected, but back home at her parents' house. As we talked, she confessed how much she hated her new college and how much she missed home. When I told her about our dilemma, she said she wished she could be Carson's preschool teacher. I said, "Maybe you can."

By that afternoon, Amy had withdrawn from the faraway college—a spiritual surrender of her own—and enrolled in a local university. She moved back home, and arranged to teach preschool in a newly opened class in which we immediately enrolled Carson.

In my wildest dreams, I could not have imagined a more perfect solution!

I love this example because it exemplifies everything I believe about spiritual surrender and how we can practice it in our daily lives. This was not a life-or-death situation; it was just a simple problem that I was able to release and trust that an answer would be revealed to me. My rational mind kept trying to convince me to just keep him in the first school. Several friends, who I respect as mothers, had their children enrolled there—it must be a good school. But I couldn't deny that nagging gut feeling—my intuition telling me that this was not the right situation for my son. I'm sure this was my message from the Universe, letting me know that something better was possible, with a little faith and patience.

The synchronicities of this situation seemed miraculous. As *A Course in Miracles* says, "There is no order of difficulty in miracles. One is not 'harder' or 'bigger' than another. They are all the same."

Book of Surrender

DO YOU HAVE A DREAM? A PROBLEM? GO AHEAD. WRITE IT
DOWN, THEN CLOSE THE BOOK.

—*JILL ALTHOUSE-WOOD*

READING A GOOD BOOK is my favorite way to end the day. When
I lose myself in someone else's drama, I'm able to forget
about the dishes in the sink and my dentist appointment the next
day. When I open the book, my body relaxes. Then when I shut the
book I let go of the day and sleep.

But with morning, my life comes rushing back to me with its
doses of unfilled desires, unmet goals, and bothers that range
from petty to painful. I've learned that with these things, too, I can
transform them by "shutting the book."

The process began for me four years ago, when I saw some
dresses in a catalog. I had just given birth to my daughter and
returned from a long maternity leave. I was beginning to get back
into shape, but unfortunately our finances hadn't rebounded as
quickly as my waistline.

As much as I longed for two of the dresses, we couldn't afford
them. On a whim, I cut out the pictures of those two dresses and
pasted them in a blank book. Days later I added pictures of other
things I wanted: a garden, dogs, even a smiling girl in rainbow
tights.

Eventually I didn't care so much that the dresses weren't hanging in my closet. The fact that I pasted them into a collage gave me
ownership. I had a larger vision for myself—a sense of what I
wanted that ownership to feel like. I closed the book and forgot
about them.

A few weeks later, I heard a radio ad about a warehouse sale.
One day that week, I left work early and stopped at the warehouse,
just a few blocks away from where I had to pick up my children at

the sitter. All the clothing items at this sale were $10—a small fraction of the price of the dresses in the catalog!

Inside that warehouse I found the exact matches to the pictures in my book. I couldn't believe it. They were manufactured at that very site, one town away from where I lived and worked.

As time passed, I began to notice other things in my book materializing. What was it about putting pictures on paper that gave my ideas such power?

I realized that it wasn't the pictures or the words themselves that were carrying out my will, but that I had given my dreams a home other than my mind. I had taken them out of the worry zone and closed the book on them.

Since that time I've expanded my practice. I include questions and prayers—whatever I need the Universe to handle—in my Book of Surrender. Sometimes the answers are instant. Sometimes it takes years before I see the results.

My husband tends to discount my observations on the subject. He's a logical man who would rather believe in coincidences than the spiritual workings of the Universe.

His proof came while he was job hunting. For most of the year he had been sending out résumés with no good prospects on the horizon. I told him to write down exactly what he wanted in a job. He refused with the argument that he didn't want to box himself into such a narrow description. He was desperate to get away from his old job; he did not need an ideal.

But on a long road trip, he gave in and dictated his thoughts on his perfect job. I wrote his every specification, even when he said he wanted a job that included some time on the golf course. When we were finished, we decided to forget our jobs and enjoy our vacation.

He got the call on his cellular phone while we were 1,000 miles from home. It was a personnel director from a local company wanting him to come in for an interview. My husband now works for that company and was put in charge of the company golf league his first year.

I know why spiritual surrender is so powerful and why this

method has worked so well. The pages of my Book of Surrender became a training ground for the things I wanted to bring into reality. But I needed to let go of my hopes as outcomes and release them.

Do you have a dream? A problem? Go ahead. Write it down, then close the book.

—Jill Althouse-Wood

Faith is power. When we obsess about our problems and the things we lack, that is what will manifest in our reality. By imagining the possibilities—our positive intentions—clearly, then letting them go and having faith in the benevolence of the Universe, we remove the barriers of our limited thoughts and open the path for wonderful things to come our way.

Finding My Higher Power

ALCOHOL WAS ONCE MY ENEMY, BUT NOW IT IS JUST SOME-
THING THAT EXISTS. SOMETHING I SEE IN THE AISLES OF THE
GROCERY STORE, BECKONING TO OTHERS, BUT IT HAS NO
POWER OVER ME ANYMORE. I GAVE MY ADDICTIONS TO GOD
AND HE JUST TOOK THEM AWAY.

—*MARIE JONES*

SIX YEARS AGO, I decided to get sober.
It was not a decision I made lightly. It was a decision that came
from years of agony, pain, depression, and waste. It was a decision
that required me to do something I never thought I could find the
courage to do. I knew I couldn't do it on my own; I needed the help
of a power far greater than myself.

I had suffered from depression and anxiety since adolescence,
during a time when little was known about such problems. A history of sexual abuse and a rape had left me with scars so deep that
I often didn't even know they were there, casting their dark shad-
ows on all aspects of my life. I blamed myself, and the pain and
worthlessness I felt deep at my core led to several unsuccessful
suicide attempts.

Day after day, and night after night of despair finally led me to
seek solace in alcohol and prescription pills—whatever would take
the edge off, whatever would make me numb. If it worked, I took
it, and when that amount didn't work anymore, I took more and
more still. Before I knew it, I was an addict.

I spent most of my twenties and early thirties in a blur of action,
experience, and movement. My sole purpose in life during that
time was to feel as much and as little as possible, a contradiction
that only an addict could understand. I learned that the phrase,
"You never get enough of what you don't want," was true, as I was
never able to feel fulfilled, satisfied, or comfortable in my skin.

That longing kept me searching for more; more experiences, more excitement, more stimulation, yet, all the while, my heart was numbed to what I was feeling deep down, as if to protect me from the truth of just how sick I had become.

They say in Alcoholics Anonymous that you won't get sober until you hit bottom. I hit bottom on a sunny winter morning six years ago, when the strain of caring not just for my own out-of-control life, but for that of my equally alcoholic and desperately ill husband, finally caught up with me. After spending the morning in tears, trying to get my husband to stop drinking and to realize how sick he was, something inside me snapped. I suddenly felt as though I was not really talking to him at all, but to myself, and that I was the one who needed that realization—that I was just as sick and in need of help as my husband was.

A flood of hatred and self-loathing and rage and despair gushed from deep within me. I suffered a complete emotional breakdown, and for the first time, I revealed to another human being—my husband—the extent of my own illness and the terrible secrets of the childhood sexual abuse that had forced me to seek solace in alcohol.

I felt so dirty—all I could think of was getting into the shower and trying to wash away all the memories I had just unleashed. As I lay in a crumpled heap in the bathtub, drenched from the water of the shower, I begged God to take my past from me and let me start over again, fresh and clean and new. I prayed for forgiveness, for all the terrible abuses I had imposed upon myself as a result of my past. I also prayed for the strength to forgive those who had abused me, and release the inner rage that was threatening to destroy my hopes for a happy future.

As my body wracked with sobs, I felt something give inside of me. Only it wasn't a surrender of defeat, it was a surrender to the truth that I had been resisting and avoiding for years. I now knew I could not heal myself. I needed God.

I began to pray, meditate, and read spiritual works, and attend church for the first time in years. I had always claimed to believe in God, but realized that I had been just paying my belief lip service.

In my heart, I had always felt alone. Ask any addict and they will tell you—the reason they drank or used in the first place was to feel whole, powerful, a part of the bigger picture—all the things that only love, especially the love of God, can bring.

I began to feel a connection with something deeper and far grander than what my own eyes could see—something that permeated all of life and all of me. I began to sense that this "something" was what my soul had been seeking all along, before it got lost along the path and found the poor substitutes of drugs and alcohol.

One day at a time, one minute at a time, I purged the darkness within me and opened up a space to let the light back in.

God not only heard my prayer of surrender, but my husband's as well. He, too, became active in AA and faced his own denials and sickness with newfound faith, strength, and determination. We pledged to ourselves that we would overcome our addictions with our love for each other and with God's help.

Now I know I am never alone. For I have found the only thing there is that can really fill us, satisfy us, love us, and make us whole. It is not a substance, or a material object. It is not anything one can see or hear or feel on the physical plane. It is so much more than that.

I found my Higher Power, a God who loved and cared for me always and forever, and I found it in the last place I expected to, right where I left it—within.

—Marie Jones

God is always there for us, waiting to hear the awful truths that we feel we must keep secret inside ourselves. God is always there to love us, no matter what our past. We can surrender our biggest problems and know they will be healed through the power of love.

A Shadow of Faith

FAITH MEANS BEING GRASPED BY A POWER THAT IS
GREATER THAN WE ARE, A POWER THAT SHAKES US
AND TURNS US, AND TRANSFORMS AND HEALS US.
SURRENDER TO THIS POWER IS FAITH.

—*PAUL TILLICH*

IT SEEMED A LOGICAL IDEA to get cats for the barn after we moved into a house on a farm. It was especially important for our son, Kyle, who'd already had two sad experiences with kittens that died soon after he had gotten them. It became Kyle's quest to have a kitten.

We began our search for two brother kittens—one for Kyle and one for his little brother, Daniel. In that late autumn, the colored leaves were plentiful and the pecan trees around our house were full of squirrels, but no kittens could be found. We looked in the newspaper, on the community bulletin boards, and at the vet's office. Still, no kittens.

One night, as we knelt by the beds to say prayers, Daniel, with the perfect faith of a child, asked God to help the kittens to find us. This surprised me, who usually felt compelled to use my own resources and tenacity to solve problems. Daniel's solution was far more effective, for find us, the kittens did.

In the next Friday newspaper, the thing we had searched for (almost) was there. The advertisement read: "Two free kittens found on the side of the road." Who could resist unwanted, un-loved orphans? We called right away.

I had never seen such pathetic little bundles of fur. When I saw Bert and Tiger, I had to wonder if their appearances were a result of their roadside abandonment or the cause of it.

Their heads were much too large for their skeletal bodies and their eyes were matted with goo. One of them meowed incessantly, as if the sound of her own voice would reassure her that she was still alive. The other was silent, ever cautious, looking for some reason to hide. We brought them home with us; of course, ignoring the fact that they were sister kittens, rather than the brothers we'd hoped to find.

Kyle and Daniel only saw potential as I mentally calculated the vet bill for ensuring their survival. The kittens thrived, much to the surprise of everyone except my sons.

By the time they were not kittens anymore, they were firmly entrenched in our lives and hearts. It didn't take long to see that each cat had taken on the personality of her owner: Tiger, Kyle's cat, was sweet-natured and affectionate, happy to please; Bert was more like Daniel—quick, feisty, and unpredictable.

Then one day Bert came home dragging her leg and meowing pitifully, obviously in pain. I took her to the vet and was dismayed to find that her leg was full of birdshot.

After a long confinement and much suffering on her part, she survived, and lives to this day . . . albeit with a limp that will never go away.

Tiger, Kyle's cat, never came home. We had to face the possibility that she had not been as lucky as Bert. Kyle was heartbroken. He called and called for Tiger. He searched the woods and creek banks for her. The thought that she was hurt somewhere and needed his help haunted him.

As the days passed and we saw no sign of Tiger, Kyle had to allow the truth to seep in that she would not be coming home. He tried to be brave, but to lose three cats in a row was more than a little boy could bear. He said he never wanted another pet, not for the rest of his life.

Hoping he would change his mind, I began to gently plant seeds to make him receptive to trying once more. Eventually, he said that he would give it one last try.

But, this time, he made very specific stipulations about the sort of kitten he would accept. It was as if he thought if he made it hard enough to find a certain kind of kitten, he never would, and he wouldn't have to risk hurt again.

He told me he wanted a kitten *only if* it could be a boy and black without a single white hair. This time we began our search with a prayer for the kitty to find us, just like before with Bert and Tiger. I had learned my lesson.

I thought it would be just as easy as before. We would pray, and in a few days we would find a black kitten, just like a road sign, painted by God himself.

But, this time, it didn't happen. We searched and spread the word to everyone that we wanted a black kitten but none could be found. Kyle was firm in his requirements not to settle for any kitten other than the one he "ordered." At times I tried to sway him to accept kittens that were available and ready to be adopted, but he was resolved.

I tried to suggest to him that we might not find the "perfect kitten" for him. But in trying to cushion his disappointment, I was taking away the one thing that he needed more than anything, even more than a kitten—his faith. He needed faith that there was someone bigger than us all who watched over him and his kitten tragedies. He needed to believe that his loss was not an insignificant thing to be overlooked by the God who coordinates the universe and every living thing in it. He needed to know that the God who never fails to see a sparrow fall is the same God who cared that he was sad and knew he needed a touch from his Heavenly Father.

The answer came in the most unexpected way and was one of the most powerful lessons I have had in all my years of seeking God. It is fitting that I was led to it through a little boy whose faith was much bigger than mine.

Many days after the beginning of our search for the black kitten, the phone rang. On the line was our neighbor, Betty. Her husband, Pete, had been making his daily walk. On this walk, he found a kitten and brought it home to Betty who knew we were looking for one.

I held my breath as I turned to Kyle and said, "Pete has found a stray kitten on the road. Do we want to give it a home?"

He weighed the question thoughtfully. After a time, he shrugged and said, "We may as well."

I reassured Kyle that we would keep looking for his "perfect" kitten, that this didn't mean we were giving up. We'd just have *two* kittens instead of one. He just listened quietly. When I finished my speech, he said, "Did she say what color it was?" I hadn't even bothered to ask.

When we arrived, Pete sat on his porch and held something tiny in his weathered hands. Kyle walked purposefully ahead, shoulders straight as he approached. Then he saw the kitten! It was a male and black, without a single white hair anywhere!

Kyle named him Shadow, and for many years, he was that very thing.

I learned a valuable lesson . . . that faith is perfected in patience. In surrender, we find grace and love so abundant that it spills over into the tiniest details or the smallest of God's creatures. Sometimes when we look so hard to find something ourselves, the love of God creeps up behind us in the most unexpected and delightful ways, like a kitten's paws in damp grass.

—Sarah Holcombe

It is said that a problem not worth praying about is not worth worrying about. Even the smallest problem is an opportunity to experience the miraculous when surrendered to God.

The Prodigal Daughter

GOOD PARENTS GIVE THEIR CHILDREN ROOTS AND WINGS.
ROOTS TO KNOW WHERE HOME IS, WINGS TO FLY AWAY
AND EXERCISE WHAT'S BEEN TAUGHT THEM.
—JONAS SALK

I'VE BEEN PREACHING the words of the Bible most of my life, but there's one point on which I disagree with the teachings of Jesus. I believe the Prodigal Son was not a boy, but a girl, and my own daughter is the reason.

When Patty was a baby, we looked at her with the wonder of new parents, and said proudly, "She's going to be her own individual!" We didn't realize just what that would mean and how much pain it would cause for all of us.

My wife and I raised her in the church; she was involved in all of the children's activities and was a leader on the Youth Council, taking part in several Mission Trips. The other parents pointed to Patty as an example for their own kids. We were so proud of her.

But, a few years later, in late December, our single, independent eighteen-year-old college-student daughter presented us with a Christmas present that broke our hearts: She was pregnant.

We should have seen it coming.

We'd had the usual parent-teenager struggles at home, and when Patty finally graduated high school, she set out to conquer her world. Up until that point, we'd held her pretty close, always providing a "safety net" for her. That summer after graduation, we allowed her the freedom of being an adult, without a net to catch her. Like the son in the parable, Patty just wanted to do her own, rebellious thing. But, unlike the son, she stayed at home. I was amazed at how things went so badly so quickly.

The boy that Patty was involved with was a high school dropout who was into drugs. He had a violent temper, especially when he was high, and he took his anger out on Patty.

He dominated every aspect of her life—from the clothes she wore to telling her where to be and when, no matter what the hour. And, if she didn't respond exactly as he said, there was usually a price for her to pay. She went through a transformation from a strong, independent girl to a manipulated child right before our eyes.

In the beginning we tried to accept the young man and include him in our family, just as we have with all our children's friends. But, when things kept getting worse, we knew we had to take a stand.

We talked with Patty calmly about what love is and how it should be demonstrated. We argued with her over God's plan for her and our desires for her. We yelled in frustration at our inability to understand why she would want this trouble in her life. We even issued ultimatums and threats, but, no matter what we tried, we were helpless to change anything. I wondered, "How could things have gotten so out of control?" We had tried so hard to be good parents and do all the right things.

The days following our discovery of her pregnancy were turbulent. Word had already begun to get out among the congregation; several people knew about it before we did. Some of the members felt that I should resign as pastor since I "couldn't control my family." I was angry, embarrassed, ashamed, afraid, and confused.

As a pastor, I've worked with a lot of parents. Some abused their kids, others abandoned their kids, and some never taught morals to their kids because they could not teach what they did not know. And yet, their kids turned out okay! I'd tried to be a good parent, and thought I was doing a pretty good job. Why was God allowing my child's future to be destroyed?

One night, before the baby was born, we had a disagreement with Patty that changed everything. Decisions needed to be made about what to do next. Should they marry? Would she keep the baby or give it up for adoption? For us and for Patty, abortion was out of the question. This was the only point at which she agreed with us despite the objections of the father-to-be. My wife and I offered several options, but Patty didn't want any of them, and her options were unacceptable to us. We were at a stalemate, and neither side would budge. We ended up in a heated argument, and Patty left the house in the middle of the night.

On this night, I wept like I'd never wept before. My grief was so great that I could hardly bear it. I was crushed and defeated as I realized that I'd lost my "little girl," perhaps forever.

When she walked out that door, I understood the grief of the father in the parable when he thought his son was dead. At that moment I was willing to do almost anything just to get Patty to come back home. I wanted to know that she was safe. I wanted to protect her from the violence and ugliness of the world. I wanted things to be normal. I wanted her to come back home.

My grief lasted for days, as we hadn't heard from Patty and didn't know where she was. It was then I turned to the parable of the Prodigal Son in the Gospels, looking for comfort. Instead, I found wisdom and direction.

In the parable, the father didn't chase after the son or try to find out where he was staying or what he was doing. In fact, the father treated the son as if he were dead. With the help of the older son, the father continued to run the daily operations of the farm. I'm sure the Prodigal Son was constantly on his mind, as Patty was constantly on my mind. But, he allowed the son to learn on his own from his own experiences. In the end, the younger son eventually returns home with a much better attitude than the older son who stayed at home.

As I read that parable, I realized that if Patty came back home right away, nothing would be different. I had to completely remove my safety net for Patty and allow her to learn on her own. But how can a loving parent ever completely let go of their child? It was one of the most difficult things I've ever done, but I knew it was the right thing to do. The Prodigal Son only "came to himself" after he was in the pen with the pigs sifting through the slop for his own food.

Through that parable, God showed me what I needed to do. I had to let go of my daughter and trust that he would work in her life. My prayer changed from "Lord, bring her home" to "Lord, help her get to the pigpen quickly."

It's true what God says in Romans 8:28: "All things work together for the good for them that love the Lord." It's now been four years since we first heard the news that our daughter was pregnant. Patty went to a maternity home, chose to keep the baby and lose the boyfriend. My precious granddaughter now calls me "Paw-Paw."

Patty eventually made it to the pigpen, without any help from me. I won't say we killed the fatted calf and lived happily ever after —not yet, anyway. But, Patty is much more mature and stronger now, because she knows there's no safety net under her if she falls. It's changed her perspective on life, and she's now dealing with the consequences of her own choices. She's learning to make her own way, and I'm learning to watch from the sidelines.

Her mother and I still don't always agree with many of the decisions that Patty makes, but she doesn't ask us to agree. There is a road that God has stretched out before her, but it's her journey, not mine. But like in the parable, my daughter, whom I once thought was dead, is alive. We visit together regularly, and I get to be "Paw-Paw" a lot.

I have felt the grief of the father in the parable. Yet, I also felt his joy when the wayward child returns home. When the time was right, the father of the Prodigal Son let him go to learn on his own. It was only in letting my daughter go that we both were able to grow. I learned that you cannot hold onto your adult kids too tightly. She learned to catch herself when she falls.

—John D. Ashworth

One of the most painful experiences in life is watching someone we love act in what we perceive to be a self-destructive way—especially when that someone is one of our children. We want to protect them, to keep them from making mistakes—maybe the same mistakes that we have made—and rescue them from their troubles. We can advise, help, and support our loved ones, but we cannot control their actions. We have to learn to let go of our struggle to control them—even when we think it's for their own good. When we allow them to use their wings to travel along their own paths, learn their own lessons, and take responsibility for their own lives, we also give them the freedom and safety to return home.

Praying for My Enemy

THE GREATEST HERO IS HE WHO MAKES HIS ENEMY HIS FRIEND.

—*THE TALMUD*

I GLANCED AT RACHEL, my coworker, and frowned. "Here we go again," I said. "I wish he'd move faster and get over here. I think he actually goes into slow motion when it's time to do something for us. I've had it with him. We're losing money by the minute!" She sighed, nodding in agreement.

We worked in a hot, oily factory where we assembled brake hoses for many of the major auto manufacturers. Before we could box the completed assemblies and push them down the conveyor to the inspector and to the shipping department, we needed to date-stamp each hose. But before we could do that, Jim, our set-up man, needed to change our stamper to the current date. The sooner he did, the sooner we could complete our parts. Because we were paid by the finished piece, those hoses were dollar signs to us; the more we completed, the more money we made.

As soon as we got to the factory, we were eager to get to work, and we had to start assembling hoses, whether or not our date stamper was ready. When we had to wait, we had to pile the completed but unstamped hoses into big, awkward canvas baskets. The minutes often turned into hours as we worked, filled those baskets, and waited for Jim. And we fumed. When he finally changed our stamper, we'd have to stop assembling and go back to stamp each hose, taking more time and energy than if we'd stamped them as we went along. This meant we'd earn less money.

We didn't know why he made us wait so long each day. Jim had to change all the stampers every morning, but we noticed that others around us didn't wait as long as we did. Yet, it seemed the worse our attitudes became, the longer it took him to work his way over to us. It soon became a vicious cycle. We waited and we got angry. We then threw our parts into baskets; we waited some more, and we grew even angrier.

I knew Rachel was upset and I had no control over her feelings. However, what began to trouble me was—*me*. I knew my attitude was terrible. I was badmouthing Jim and, I'm sorry to say, enjoying it. I didn't feel good about myself, and I felt like Rachel and I were just feeding off of each other's anger—making the situation worse.

So one day, while driving to work, I realized I could do something to change our circumstances. I would lift Jim up in prayer every morning, even before entering the factory. I had believed Jim was stealing my peace, joy, and finances. I considered him my enemy. The Bible says, "Love your enemies, do good to them. . . ." So, with God's help, I vowed to love him and be kind to him. However, it did not end there. God needed to do a work in my life, as well, and I had to allow him to do that. So, I prayed also for my heart and attitude to change. God answered my prayer.

Before long, we started to see a pleasant change in Jim. He began coming over to us earlier in the morning. Soon, we became his first priority for the day—without our asking—and he seemed eager to help us. We started to have friendly chats with him, and he enjoyed our company. Occasionally, he even volunteered to bring us coffee. We were no longer held up by piling our parts in baskets, and we began making more money than ever.

Soon, Jim became our friend, and we looked forward to his warm smile and corny jokes. From that time on, until he retired, we had a wonderful working relationship.

Now, as I look back, I am so glad I prayed for Jim—and me. That same Bible verse continues, "Then your reward will be great. . . ." Because I took time to pray for both my enemy and myself, I did receive a great reward—God's peace and a bigger paycheck.

—Donna J. Werstler

A miracle is a change in our perception—the decision to love instead of hate, to work with, instead of against. When dealing with those who are difficult to love, we can always ask for help in opening our hearts. When we change our thoughts from attack to love, miracles flow freely in ways we would never had thought possible.

No More Running

I'M A RUNNER. WHEN THINGS GET DIFFICULT, I RUN. BUT I'VE
HAD ENOUGH OF MAKING BAD DECISIONS. I'VE GIVEN UP
RUNNING.

—*SUNEE SHELBY*

I LAY NAKED ON THE FLOOR in a motel room in Las Vegas that
smelled like a mix of sweat, smoke, and urine. The curtains were
drawn—as they had been for the past three days—and I was surrounded by overflowing ashtrays and my own torn clothes. I
throbbed inside and out with a dull pain, clouded by the massive
amount of methamphetamines in my body. This time, I *knew* I
would turn my life around. As usual, I was about to run, but this
time I was running in the right direction.

I'd tried to give up my addictions before, but my resolve never
stuck. The drugs were an escape hatch out of my pain. But things
were different this time. I had finally hit bottom—the lowest depth
of fear, shame, and self-loathing.

My life was not easy, almost from the start. I was born thirty-five
years ago to a Korean mother and an American G.I. father. My father
held me once and then walked out on my mother and me forever.
When I was ten months old, I contracted polio, and forever lost the
use of my legs. My mother lived with her parents, who scorned me
as a half-breed, which meant that I was less than nothing in the
Korean culture. With little money and an unsupportive family, taking care of a disabled child was too difficult for my mother, so she
put me up for adoption. I was on a plane from Korea to the United
States by myself when I was three and a half years old. I never saw
my mother again. Later, I discovered she committed suicide.

I was adopted by a nice family, and I had a good childhood, but
something always felt like it was missing. I didn't feel worthy of
anything good in my life.

I got pregnant when I was nineteen, got married, and gave birth to three daughters in six years. My husband was abusive, and I was lonely and unhappy, but I couldn't see any way out. Then my neighbor said, "Have you ever tried speed?" The moment I tried it my life was immediately, drastically different. It was great! I had energy to get things done, I lost weight without trying, and, most important, I didn't have to hurt anymore.

I started selling dope, since I knew where all the drugs in my neighborhood were. The more I sold, the more I did, because you need energy, because people are calling you at three in the morning, and you can't be asleep during business calls. I was smoking crank, which is more addictive than snorting it, and I got up to an eight-ball a day.

I was so busy that I wasn't even focusing on the things that were real. My marriage fell apart, but I didn't care. Drugs numbed my true feelings—helped me push them aside. Nothing really hurts when you're on speed, but, then again, nothing feels really good, either.

Eventually, I left my husband, got married to a different guy, and moved into a bigger home, a nicer neighborhood. I stopped using drugs, not realizing the drugs weren't my problem—they were just the behavior I was using to escape the problem.

I was still lonely and I still felt worthless. The new husband, the new house, the new stuff—were all just external Band-Aids for the wounds that I felt inside. I had everything I thought I ever wanted, and I was still miserable. I had a nervous breakdown, and then I ran—this time to Las Vegas with another man.

I didn't tell anyone where I was going—even my children didn't know where I was. I was in such a state of hopelessness that it didn't occur to me that they needed me. I soon started doing drugs again and got heavier and heavier into them. I was in Vegas for a year and a half, and by the end of that time, I was a mess—crying all the time. I found out that that my daughters had ended up in the foster care system, and the guilt overwhelmed me. I didn't think I could ever go back. I didn't think I could make up for what I had done, so I thought I would just stay away forever.

When I was almost at bottom, a friend of mine called the children's grandfather—my ex-husband's father, who had always been kind to me. He told me he'd send me a bus ticket home if I promised to get straightened out. Desperate, I promised, but I wasn't sure if I could trust my own word.

Because I'm in a wheelchair, I had to make an advance reservation for a bus with the right equipment to accommodate my chair, so I had a few days before I could leave. I moved out of my apartment and checked into a motel. The boyfriend that I had left my husband for had left me, so I was alone. I decided I was going to party, so I spent all the money I had left—about $440—to buy a huge amount of drugs. I was going to smoke it all and go out high! I was going to blast my way out of Las Vegas with one last fling.

That binge ended abruptly in the worst night of my life. After I checked into the motel, for three days straight there were people in my room—not really friends, just people pretending to be my friends because I was throwing the party of the century. We were so high, we broke our pipe, and we were smoking crank out of a light bulb.

On my last night in Vegas I found myself alone in the room, stoned, with some strange guy. That's when he raped me.

I remember what he said to me: "You asked for this—don't be surprised. You can't stop it now. There's no going back."

And that's how I felt—like I asked for it. I felt so angry and afraid and ashamed. That's when I *knew* I was going to change my life.

When I got to the bus, they had lost my reservation. They told me I couldn't get on the bus—that they didn't have the equipment to load my wheelchair. But I was determined. "I am getting on that bus," I said. "I'll crawl on that bus if I have to." I ended up using the luggage lift to get on the bus. I knew I had to get out of Vegas or my life would be over.

When I got home, the children's grandfather helped me get a placement in a Christian homeless shelter for women and children. Here, I'm learning to be the way that God created me. I've learned that we take our issues, personalities, and our quirks and we stuff part of it, we justify part of it, and we vent the rest of it in all the wrong ways. Here, we're learning to get the ugly out—sometimes things that we've kept secret all of our lives—things we don't even like to admit to ourselves. We let it go, sort through it. We give it to God, and the healing begins.

I always knew that I would stop *using* drugs, but I never even thought there was a possibility of *not wanting* the drugs. I had been using drugs for six years, and I prayed that just the thought of using again would disgust me. I gave it all up to God. I've been here over a year now, and I can honestly say that my desire for drugs is gone—I was delivered. I didn't just want to be abstinent—that's the worst, because then you're just "not doing drugs," but that hole inside you is always there waiting to be filled. I filled that void inside myself with truth and with love.

The most amazing miracle of all is that I got my children back. I was able to sit with them, cry with them, and ask them to forgive me.

From the time I came back into their lives, my kids always said, "Mom, I forgive you," but I don't think it meant anything at first. It's taken a year and a half of counseling and talking and crying and yelling and being angry—and learning God's acceptance.

The real turning point came a few weeks ago. We were all sitting on the bed, looking at photo albums that my biological mother had given to my adoptive mother, and that she had recently given to me. As we looked at the pictures together, the girls got very emotional, very sad, quiet. And I said, "This is it, girls. I understand what it's like," and the tears came. We had all felt abandoned and rejected. We had all been given up by mothers. We knew what it was like to have the ultimate hurt.

I think the key phrase was to say, "I understand. I've been through it, too." For me to actually ask my children to forgive me instead of just saying, "I'm sorry." My youngest daughter crawled into my lap and just started loving me, and I knew everything would be okay. Forgiveness is the key, and forgiveness has set us free. I no longer need to escape. I'm done running.

—Sunee Shelby

Spiritual surrender is giving up all the hurt, shame, and bad decisions we've made in the past. No matter what we've done, we give
up our problems, and, in an instant, we are free to begin anew.

An Incredible Miracle

I USED TO THINK SPIRITUAL SURRENDER MEANT PUTTING OUT
A WHITE FLAG AND GIVING UP. WHAT IT MEANS TO ME NOW IS
BEING ABLE TO PREPARE AND PLAN FOR WHATEVER IT IS I
WANT AND NEED IN MY LIFE, AND THEN TO RELEASE THE OUT-
COME, AND LET THE VERY BEST OUTCOME COME THROUGH
WITHOUT REALLY KNOWING WHAT THAT WILL BE.

—JULIE JOHNSON

WHEN MY SON, Russ, was seventeen, I got the call from the hospital that all mothers fear. It was senior skip day, and Russ had been swimming at a lake with his buddies. He dove in and hit the bottom and broke his neck.

I rushed to the hospital and saw my big, athletic son lying perfectly still on the floor with sandbags around his neck. The doctor warned that he must not move, or he could die.

He showed me the X ray. It had this big dark spot on it, and the doctor said, "That dark spot is pressure, and we have to operate to remove it. If we don't remove the pressure, he's going to die, but when we do remove the pressure, he's going to become a quadriplegic."

The doctor said this right in front of my son, and when he heard it, he said, "Mom, if I'm gong to be a quadriplegic, I'd rather die. Let me die." He was a jock, and that destiny was unimaginable to him.

Of course, I couldn't just let him die, so, I said, "Russ, what if we have an incredible miracle here? What if you don't have to be a quadriplegic and you don't have to die? That's what I would go for, how about you?"

He said nothing, so I just let it go. I didn't call anyone. I didn't want to bring anyone else's anxiety and fear into the situation. For two hours I just sat on the floor and read *Road and Track* to him while we waited for the neurologist, who was being flown in from Stanford University.

When the doctor arrived, I told Russ, "I'm going to go home now and meditate because I know that you're going to have a complete healing. The doctor's going to come in, he's going to remove the pressure, and you're not going to become a quadriplegic." I was convinced that that was the outcome, but I surrendered to the Universe whatever would happen.

When I got up to leave, I put my hand to his face and he kissed the palm of my hand, kind of like a man does to a woman. And he said, "I love you, Mom," and when he said that a tear rolled down his cheek.

He was such a macho kid, and I never saw him cry. I was so shocked by that, I touched the tear, and said, "I love you, too, honey."

Instantly I felt an energy that went through us that was so unbelievably powerful. I felt like I had my hand in an electric socket. I pulled it away because I didn't want him to see me cry and think that I didn't believe he could be healed.

I walked out of the room and went home. I was in meditation about two minutes, when the phone rang. It was the doctor and he said, "You know what, these miracles happen with kids and we don't know how they happen. I took him in again for more X rays, and the pressure was gone from his spine, so we don't have to operate. We're going to put a head brace on him and send him home."

I had been convinced that the operation would do it, but it happened without the operation. I had a goal, we were bringing in the best neurosurgeon in the country and he was going to operate. That was my goal, but I released the outcome. I had absolute conviction that he was going to be well, and that all I had to do was sit there with him calmly and read that *Road and Track*.

Miracles are about surrendering. I don't think people have this power. I think it's that when we surrender, we open ourselves to the presence of love, and it's love that heals.

—Julie Johnson

When we let go of our ideas about how things should happen, trust God, and act with love, we experience miracles.

A Large Place

ACT BOLDLY AND UNSEEN FORCES WILL COME TO YOUR AID.

—DOROTHEA BRANDE

YEARS AGO, when our children were toddlers, my husband, Roger, brought home brochures about Mammoth Cave, Kentucky. He was dancing like a big kid over the prospect of visiting there. But there was a problem. I battled claustrophobia—especially in dark caves.

My fear of tight places started at age five when I was exploring my grandfather's garage. I had climbed into an empty storage cabinet, and then shut the door that wedged tightly closed. Although I was only in the cabinet for 30 minutes before being found, it felt like hours to me. I pounded, shoved the door, and cried; the air became warm and close; I felt like I would die in that dark hole. The problem was bad enough for me to avoid elevators; if I had to ride one, I'd hold my breath and close my eyes. I hadn't told Roger, and he hadn't noticed.

I suggested a fishing weekend. Roger frowned, then waved the brochures at me. "Look how cool this cave is!" He watched as I looked at the photos, eyes hopeful.

How could I say no to his baby blues? Gulping at the lump of fear, I reasoned with myself, "How tight can a cave called Mammoth be?"

"Okay, but you're in charge of the kids," I agreed.

Inside the cave's massive entrance, illuminated brightly with electric lights, air currents rushed past. The vast openness and refreshing breeze on the hot day gave me a feeling of false confidence. "This is easy. What was such a big deal?" I thought.

Walking through the huge underground rooms awed me. Stalactites created fantasy images while swirled patterns etched on ceilings.

Deeper we went, pausing to admire formations. Then we entered a small side cave and the guide turned off all the lights. My pulse hammered in overdrive. Cold sweat beaded my forehead. The guide sounded a million miles away. Claustrophobia had struck!

I grabbed Roger's arm, pressed close, and stage-whispered in his ear, "Get-me-out-of-here!"

When the lights came up a surprised, red-faced stranger had permanent imprints of my fingernails in his arm. The poor fellow cleared his throat. I let go, and then turned away, frantically searching for Roger. He was kneeling a few feet away, his arms protecting our kids, who'd been frightened by the dark.

I stomped to his side. "Where did you go?" I shouted, mad and scared.

Roger calmed me down—for a while. Then we came to a section of the cave called "Fat Man's Squeeze." Even the name scared me!

Feeling adventurous, Roger was more than ready. "Let's go!" he said with a big grin, kids in tow, leading the way. I hesitated, my imagination conjuring up images of getting lost, of ceilings and walls closing in when I triggered the action by stepping on a hidden button. For a second my feet seemed stuck in quick-dry wet cement. "Maybe I should just turn around and go back to the car," I thought. I looked over my shoulder, then back at Roger already a few feet into the tunnel.

The return path to our car was circuitous, long, and often dark. We'd been walking in the cave for more than 45 minutes by then. The rest of our cave tour group had all opted to push on, and now they waited on me to step into the tunnel. Some were getting ugly about it. "Get a move on, woman!" one man shouted harshly. I had no choice but to follow Roger.

On first entering the tunnel, the footpath easily held two people. However, it quickly narrowed to single file, heel to toe. Finally, I was completely hunched over, my breath more shallow with each step as my shoulders brushed the cave's walls.

Suddenly I froze in place, suffocation blanketing me. My vision blurred in the dim tunnel and my head spun. I was back in that cabinet at age five again. I screamed, "Roger! I can't breathe! I'm going to die!"

With our son in the crook of one arm, daughter hanging on his back, he reached for me with his free hand. Holding my shaking, icy hands, he gently pulled me forward. "Come on, honey," he coaxed.

At first moving was impossible. Twentysome people behind waited and muttered, stooped in awkward positions. Finally, I closed my eyes, and Roger repeated over and over, "Just one more step." I imagined Jesus leading me, holding my hand, even carrying me.

At last we entered a vast underground room four stories high. I collapsed shakily onto a bench. Roger hovered near, leaning down to ask, "Are you okay?" He laid his pocket Bible on my lap.

I leafed through the pages trying to forget the suffocation of the tunnel. Then Psalm 118:5 leaped from the page: "The Lord answered me [and set me] in a large place."

I looked around the immense room in awe. Far from home, God had sent the perfect word of comfort.

Healing laughter bubbled up as I prayed, "Lord, help me keep my steps on your narrow path and my eyes on eternity. Hold my hand. I give you my claustrophobia."

I left it that day in Mammoth Cave.

—JoAnn Reno Wray

Dear God, I give you my fears, my doubts, my sorrows, my past. Give me the courage to live each day as you would have me live—free, loving, and fearless. Amen

In Search of a Miracle

PEACE DOTH NOT DWELL IN OUTWARD THINGS, BUT
WITHIN THE SOUL; WE MAY PRESERVE IT IN THE MIDST
OF THE BITTEREST PAIN, IF OUR WILL REMAINS FIRM
AND SUBMISSIVE. PEACE IN THIS LIFE SPRINGS FROM
ACQUIESCENCE, NOT IN AN EXEMPTION FROM SUFFERING.
—*FRANÇOIS FÉNELON*

THE DAY MY FATHER was diagnosed with inoperable lung cancer, I decided to find him a miracle. My family had already spent a good part of that September chasing medical options, and what we had discovered was not hopeful. Given the odds, a miracle cure was our best and most reasonable hope.

We are a superstitious family, skeptical of medicine and believers in omens, potions, and the power of prayer. The week that the first X ray showed a spot on my father's lung, three of us had dreams that could be read as portents.

I dreamed of my maternal grandmother, Mama Rose. My cousin, whose own father had died when she was only two and who had grown up next door to us, with my father stepping in as a surrogate parent for her, dreamed of our great-uncle Rum. My father dreamed of his father for the first time since he'd died in 1957. All of these ghosts had one thing in common—they were happy.

For the next month my father underwent CAT scans and oscopies of all sorts, until, finally, a surgeon we hardly knew shouted across the hospital waiting room: "Where are the Woods?" "Hood," I said. "Over here." He walked over to us and without any hesitation said, "He's got cancer. A fair-sized tumor that's inoperable. We can give him chemo, buy a little time. Your doctor will give you details."

Whenever someone died in our family, my father would pull out his extra-large bottle of Jack Daniels. It had gotten us through the news of the death of my cousin's husband, my brother's accidental death in 1982, and the recent deaths of two of my fortysomething cousins. That late September afternoon, my father pulled out the bottle for his own grim prognosis. As the day wore on, we'd gotten more news: only an aggressive course of chemotherapy and radiation could help, and even then the help would be short-lived, if it came at all.

At 6'1" and more than 200 pounds, cracking jokes about the surgeon, my father did not look like someone about to die. He was not someone I was going to let die. If medical science could only give him a year and a half tops, then there was only one real hope for a cure. "There's a place in New Mexico with miracle dirt," I announced. "I'm going to go and get you some."

"Well," my father said with typical understatement, "I guess I can use all the help I can get."

For some people, perhaps, the notion of seeking a miracle cure is tomfoolery, futile, or even a sign of pathetic desperation. To believe in miracles, and certainly to go and look for one, you must put aside science and rely only on faith.

For me, that leap was not a difficult one. My great-grandmother, who died when I was six, healed people of a variety of ailments with prayer and household items, such as silver dollars and Mazola oil. I grew up with stories of miracle healings, and I never questioned them.

I had also reached a point in my life where I believed in a graced world. I believed that the birth of my son was miraculous; that the love I shared with my husband and my ability to shape words into meaningful stories were gifts. It was this faith in miracles that led me up into the mountains an hour northwest of Santa Fe, New Mexico, to the little town of Chimayo and its El Santuario. The area had been a holy ground for the Tewa Indians, who went there to eat mud when they wanted to be cured. There is a chapel built around a hole, called *el pocito* (the well) that is said to contain the healing dirt.

When I arrived at El Santuario, I had the fear of my father's death to motivate me and an open heart, a willingness to believe that a cure—a miracle—was possible. What I found in the church was testimony to all the cures attributed to this place. The walls were lined with crutches and canes, candles and flowers, statues of saints, all offerings of thanks for healings. In the small room of the *pocito,* I began to tremble. I felt I was in a holy place, a place that held possibility. I had not felt that sense of possibility in the hospital and doctors' waiting rooms that had recently dominated my life.

I kneeled in front of the *pocito* and scooped the dirt with my bare hands into the plastic bag I'd brought. I had one prayer that I had repeated over and over: "Please let my father's tumor go away."

When I arrived back in Rhode Island with the dirt from El Santuario, I felt that anything could happen. Twenty-four hours after my father held the dirt, he was in respiratory failure and was rushed to the hospital by ambulance. It was Christmas Eve, three months after his diagnosis. Although it would have been a crisis of faith, quite the opposite happened. I simply believed that he would survive. What happened next surprised me more than his bad turn of health.

While he was in the hospital, his recovery from what was diagnosed as pneumonia deemed unlikely, his doctor performed a CAT scan, assuming the tumor had grown. Doctors had said that my father would need five treatments of chemo before there would be any hope of the tumor shrinking, and he'd had only two. Visiting him, I asked if he was prepared for the CAT scan.

"Oh, no," he said with great confidence, "the tumor is gone."

"Gone?" I said.

He nodded. "I sat here and watched as the cancer left my body. It was black and evil-looking and came out of my chest like sparks, agitated and angry." I was willing to believe a tumor might disappear, but such a physical manifestation was more than I had considered.

The next day my mother called me from the hospital. "Ann," she said, awed, "the CAT scan shows that the tumor has completely gone. It's disappeared." In the background I heard my father chuckling, and then my mother made the doctor repeat what he had said when he walked into the room with the results: "It's a miracle."

Here is the part where I would like to say that my father came home, tumor-free, cancer-free, miraculously cured. The part where I would like to tell you that, well again, he traveled with me to New Mexico, to El Santuario de Chimayo, to leave his CAT scan results in the little low-ceilinged room beside the notes of thanks and crutches and braces and statues and candles.

Instead, my father went home, and the next day was once again rushed by ambulance to the hospital in respiratory failure. He died a week later from pneumonia he'd caught because of a compromised immune system.

More than once since then I have found myself wondering not if I got a miracle, but whether I had prayed for the wrong thing. Should I have bent over the *pocito* and asked for my father to live rather than for the tumor to go away? What I am certain of is this: I got exactly what I prayed for on that December afternoon at El Santuario de Chimayo.

Almost a year to the day that my father died, I went back to El Santuario de Chimayo. Father Roca, who has been the parish priest there for forty years, talked to me in his tiny office in his church.

"I have read your letter many times," he told me. "I am so happy for your family."

Thinking he was confused, I said, "But my father died."

Father Roca shrugged. "It was God's will. The tumor went away, yes?"

I nodded.

Later I returned to the room with the *pocito*. I prayed there, a prayer of thanks for the miracles that had come my way since I'd last visited Chimayo: good health, the love of my children and my husband, the closeness of my family, and, finally, the courage to accept what had come my way. If someone at the shrine on my first visit had told me the miracle I would receive was peace of mind, I would have been angry. But miracles come in many forms, both physical and spiritual.

> I remember what one visitor to Chimayo wrote, "It didn't cure me, but then it's God's will. Peace of mind is sometimes better."
>
> —Ann Hood

We cannot control all events, as hard as we may try. Even in our sorrow, peace comes with acceptance for what is and gratitude for all our blessings.

going with the flow

LORD, TAKE ME WHERE YOU WANT ME TO GO;
LET ME MEET WHO YOU WANT ME TO MEET;
TELL ME WHAT YOU WANT ME TO SAY, AND
KEEP ME OUT OF YOUR WAY.

—"MYCHAL'S PRAYER," FATHER MYCHAL F. JUDGE,
NEW YORK CITY FIRE DEPARTMENT CHAPLAIN KILLED IN THE
SEPTEMBER 11, 2001, ATTACK ON THE WORLD TRADE CENTER

*G*OING WITH THE FLOW sounds a little lazy and irresponsible to our control-oriented, rational minds. The
term conjures up images of spaced-out hippie types lying
around on beanbag chairs, reciting their mantra, "Hey, whatever."
But going with the flow is not lazy or passive; it's simply giving up
the struggle. Going with the flow means swimming—not just back-
floating aimlessly—with the current in our lives,
our intuition, our Divine guidance. Going with

THE RIVER DELIGHTS TO
LIFT US FREE, IF ONLY
WE DARE LET GO.
—RICHARD BACH,
ILLUSIONS

the flow means not exhausting ourselves trying
to force our way upstream—against nature—
and not frantically clinging to the shore—terrified of the power of the current.

So often we don't know what we truly want—
or even need—to be happy. We keep our heads
down, paddling and kicking as fast as we can in
our own direction. Often, we end up someplace we don't belong,
and wonder why we worked so hard to get there. Or we wear ourselves out and end up downstream anyway, just older, more tired,

and more resentful than we would have been if we went with the flow in the first place.

Putting a baby to sleep is a lesson in going with the flow, for both baby and parent. When my children were toddlers, they almost always fought sleep. When the word *bedtime* was uttered, my son would scrunch up his face, stiffen, and yell, "No way!' with as much enthusiasm as only a two-year-old can muster.

Then I'd carry him into his room, screaming and flailing, and sit down with him in the big, comfy rocking chair and begin the long process of helping him make peace with the night. More stiffening, a few more "No ways," and the rhythmic motion of the chair and the warm comfort of his mother would gently relax his body. He'd surrender the fight—waged only for the struggle of it—and curl up to me and let me soothe him into a blissful slumber.

Wouldn't it be wonderful if adults had someone to rock us when we're whiny, over-tired, and fretful? To take us calmly and firmly and pass their peace to us when we are struggling against the world. Like the baby who needs sleep, actually craves sleep, we often resist what's best for us.

How many times can we look back on an event that seemed like a tragedy when it happened, which turned out to be a blessing? We resist giving up our expectations, our resentments, and our busyness, yet how many times has the thing that we've been holding onto so tightly turned out to be exactly the thing we need to let go? If we only had the vision or the clarity to see the future or the lesson in the experience and trust enough to flow along with it, as the baby drifts off to sleep in the protection of his mother's arms.

We can relax into the comfort of God and let God lead us instead of forging our own way through the world. We often hear about people deciding to let God lead when they face an adversity that forces them to quit swimming upstream, change their path, and listen to their heart. People who have survived a life-threatening illness or escaped death almost always come away from the experience a changed person. When we go with the flow instead of fighting our experience, we can get to that same place with a lot less pain.

We often discover that God has a more magnificent dream for us than we had for ourselves.

IN LITTLE WHISPERS . . . YOUR INTUITION IS TELLING YOU SOME- THING. DID YOU NOT PAY ATTENTION? THE UNI- VERSE WILL SPEAK TO YOU A LITTLE LOUDER—WITH A LITTLE TAP ON THE SHOULDER. THEN YOU GET HIT IN THE HEAD BY A "BRICK." STILL NOT PAYING ATTENTION? A BRICK WALL FALLS ON YOU. STILL NOT HEAR- ING IT? THEN YOU EXPERI- ENCE A FULL-BLOWN EARTHQUAKE. —THE *OPRAH* MAGAZINE, LIVE YOUR BEST LIFE TOUR

I once heard Oprah Winfrey tell a wonderful story of letting God lead:

When she was young and just starting out, she thought she wanted to be a TV news re- porter. She was bright and good on camera, but the news was often very sad, and she found her- self empathizing with her subjects and crying on TV—not what was expected of an objective journalist.

In addition to her excessive emotion on camera, her superiors weren't happy with her looks, so they sent her to a fancy salon for a makeover. The salon put a solution on her hair that caused it to fall out, making her appearance even less appealing to her bosses, and her stress- ful reporting job even more difficult.

It was then that the news director decided that Oprah didn't have it in her to be a reporter, so she got "demoted" to a local morning talk show. Oprah says that when she did the first show, she felt like she was home—she knew that was what she was meant to do. The rest is history.

The Universe is always speaking to us, gently urging us to go with the flow. If we listen to the whispers of the Universe, we can go with the flow before the darkness hits.

Another remarkable example of letting God lead by following hints and avoiding struggle is Marcy Feit, CEO of ValleyCare, a Northern California community-centered health-care organization. Marcy began her career as a nurse's aid, and twenty-five years later found herself running the whole place. When asked about her suc- cess, she says, "People ask me if this was part of my plan. They want to know how I prepared, but I never prepared. I just came to work every day and, no matter what my title and job was, I said, 'What do I have to do? What are the problems, and how can I solve them?

How can I work to make things better?' I still do that today."

Over the years, Marcy was promoted until she had managed every area of the hospital, even though she never applied for a job. Her performance was so outstanding and her attitude so optimistic that she was asked to take on every single position—even CEO. She works hard, putting in long days, nights, and weekends, but one does not get a sense of struggle from her. She exudes calm compassion—a woman who feels confident that she is doing what she was meant to do—taking care of the health needs of her community. Today the organization that she runs is one of the few community health care entities that is operating profitably—a wonderful example of how a person can go with the flow, without controlling or manipulating— or even planning—and end up at the top of the ladder of success.

Going with the flow is not the lazy or the irresponsible way. It is the natural way to joyfully meet your greatest potential.

Wonder-uptions:
EMBRACING THE INTERRUPTED LIFE

IT IS ALWAYS THE SIMPLE THAT PRODUCES THE MARVELOUS.
—*AMELIA BARR*

BEFORE CHILDREN, my life was a lot like the many races I loved to run. I would set goals, both 10K and marathon in length, pass each mile marker at a predictable pace, and cross the finish line within a respectable time. I determined I needed three years to graduate from college, a year for an advanced degree, and increased my pace until I met these goals. My Day-Timer listed the tasks I needed to do each day, and I could, usually, check each one off as I accomplished it. I went to church weekly and loved the peace and renewal it offered. When I found out I was pregnant, I followed the advice in the books, tracked the baby's developmental milestones, ate the right foods, got the right sleep, and never forgot to take my vitamins. Certainly I had faced obstacles, much like a runner might face a cramp or a sore muscle, but I knew how to handle life's interruptions with focus and determination.

Then my daughter was born. Life was no longer a run with a steady pace. Instead it was like a horrible traffic jam. The colicky baby's cries interrupted sleep, disrupted meals, and ended showers before the shampoo was rinsed out of my hair. Goals that I'd set for myself were indefinitely put on hold. I discovered that being a mother wasn't a challenge I could meet with rational, orderly thought and planning. This was an entire new form of existence. I began to live the interrupted life.

A couple kids later I was struggling with the sense that I would never pass a single mile marker again. Life was chaotic; peace was elusive. My husband was serving in the military, constantly deployed, and we lived far from extended family. I still attended church, but it became a place of frustration when I'd have to leave with a screaming toddler on my hip and a crying baby on my shoulder. Why couldn't I complete one event or chore without interruption? Toys were everywhere, laundry was halfway into the machine, the phone rang, a child cried, macaronis boiled over on the stove. I fought it. I tried to impose order. I would dress the kids neatly, wipe their faces constantly, and follow them around picking up toys. I couldn't accept the new pace of my life and felt paralyzed while everyone seemed to be racing by.

The last straw came one night when my husband was in Somalia for five months and I'd spent the day caring for my children and answering calls from forty-two distraught wives from my husband's company. As the commander's wife, I was expected to handle rumors, problems, concerns, and complaints. It was late, the house was a mess, and I couldn't even remember if I had brushed my children's teeth before they collapsed into bed. That small negligence drove me to tears. I wanted to run . . . anywhere. Then my mother called. She patiently listened to my litany of all that I hadn't done; how I had failed miserably as a mother. She had lived through my father's two tours in Vietnam and raised four children, and I knew I probably sounded trivial to her, but if so, she didn't admit it. Instead, she asked me in a soothing voice, "Are the kids safe in their beds?"

"Well, of course," I replied.

"Did you feed them anything healthy today?"

"I guess so," I said. I thought about the leftover macaroni and cheese that was probably hardening in my sink. With a twinge of satisfaction, I remembered serving grapes and peas, too.

"Did you hug them and tell them you love them?"

"Yes, Mom. I did."

"Well then congratulations, honey. You've done a wonderful job and I'm very proud of you."

It was all I needed to hear. Guilt and self-reproach fell like an avalanche from my shoulders. I realized my expectations of how life should be run were *my* creation, and they weren't doing anybody, least of all my children, any good. I was trying to run a house full of kids like a well-orchestrated race and stumbling every step of the way. My kids weren't noticing what I was or wasn't accomplishing, but they could pick up on my frazzled attitude. If I continued to handle every interruption, whether it was phone call or spilled milk, as if it were a crisis, I would completely miss the wonder of childhood that was right in front of me.

I took a look around at my disheveled house and realized every pile and mess represented something that the children had experienced that day. They weren't all just items on my to-do list. My daughter's current obsession with picking every dandelion she passed was evident in little cups of golden drooping heads scattered all over the house. Those I wouldn't clean up. I then noticed a torn-out page of a coloring book on the floor and remembered my son's pride as he tried to interrupt a phone call and show me how he had stayed between the lines for the first time. That was a keeper. I realized that not everything that happened was a snag in my day's agenda. It was up to me to understand which interruptions warranted my attention: bee stings and scraped knees; but better, accomplishments in art or shoe tying. And, which interruptions did not: not every sibling tiff and certainly not every phone call from people whose problems I couldn't solve anyway.

I would look more deeply at those that not only merited my attention, but also revealed something about the magic of my children's lives. Those I would call "wonder-uptions." I would record them in a journal with thankfulness and would be on the alert for more of them tomorrow.

Over the years, I've filled many journals with these wonder-uptions. There was the time my son insisted on halting our shopping routine to stop in a pet store to ask for a Brontosaurus egg. And, the night my first grader called to be picked up from her first sleepover because she missed me. And another night, more recently, when that same daughter, now in middle school, sat up in bed when I went to tuck her in and wanted to talk. It was late and all I wanted was a cup of tea and a book, but a signal went off in my head. I heard a voice telling me, This isn't just a run of the mill, annoying interruption. It's a wonder-uption and deserves undivided attention. Surrender your own needs and expectations.

Embrace it.

In spite of my best efforts, with all the stops and starts involved in accomplishing one task, I still feel frustrated with the pace of parenting. It's aggravating to be late when a child can't find shoes, or to have this essay interrupted twenty-one times, or to be fixing dinner when a child drops a glass on the floor. I try to take a deep breath and ask myself if there is any sort of wonder-uption at all in the current mess. Sometimes the very thought makes me laugh so that the interruption doesn't bother me as much. And other times, the wonder is there, like a gleaming pearl waiting for me to discover and treasure it. So even though I'm not passing that many mile markers at a rabbit's pace anymore, I'm finding there is an awful lot to discover at the slower tortoise pace. The interrupted life may not be smooth striding, but I've discovered there's a lot to learn in between the stopping and starting.

—Amy Moellering

Children are our little Zen masters—forever teaching us the wonder of being in the moment, accepting what life offers. When we quit struggling with the way we think things should be and stop resisting their lessons, we can learn to appreciate the wonder-uptions of life. Wonder-uptions aren't just for parents; anytime we release our expectations of how things *should be,* we can go with the flow of *what is,* and we can appreciate the joy in even the simplest moments.

Better Than I Ever Dreamed

IF YOU TRY TO OVER-CONTROL WHAT YOU THINK YOU WILL
ACHIEVE, YOU'LL MISS WHAT YOU CAN ACTUALLY ACCOMPLISH.
—PATRICK WOLFF

TEN YEARS AGO, I got the opportunity to work with one of the best chess players in the world; he is now a World Chess Champion. That experience of looking genius in the face every day profoundly changed the way I looked at chess and life forever.

I met him at the World Junior Chess Championship. I had tied for third and he had won the tournament. We were young—I was nineteen and he was only eighteen—and, at the time, I still wasn't exactly sure what my ambitions in chess were. That's another way of saying I hadn't acknowledged any limitations to myself yet.

We had become friends, and one day he called me up and asked me to work with him to help him study for a chess tournament, so I packed my bags and flew to Spain, where he lived.

We played chess eight to ten hours per day, every day. It was very exciting for me to work with someone that good, but it was also very hard.

When our "workday" was done, we'd play blitz chess—that's where we play quickly, taking only 5 minutes each for a play, the whole game. It's a way that chess players relax. But soon he didn't want to play anymore because he would beat me all the time. I just wasn't good enough for it to be interesting to him.

It was very draining for my ego. I was angry and resentful about getting my ass whipped all the time. I was good enough to be useful to him but not good enough to be stiff competition.

Here I was doing the one thing that I cared most about in the world, the thing that I was best at, and 19 times out of 20, I would lose. The experience profoundly changed me in two ways. First, I decided that I didn't want to be a professional chess player for the rest of my life, because I could never hope to be one of the top chess players in the world and I wanted to achieve more. It was much better to start moving out of chess while I was still young and could do other things in my life.

The second thing that happened was that I honestly faced my limitations and, in doing that, became more comfortable with them. I had been seeing a shrink, and one of the issues that we were working on was my tendency to protect my ego by always leaving myself a "way out." There would always be some external reason for failure so that I could maintain the pretension that I could have done better. This experience showed me a limitation that I couldn't excuse myself out of—this guy was just a better player than I was. Although it was very painful at first, it was okay in the end. It wasn't so bad anymore to fail.

I accepted myself as I was, which, ironically, made me a much better chess player. It was then that I had the courage to compete naked—without the protective cloak of excuses I had invented for myself.

I was more able to take risks. I cared very much about every game, but I cared more honestly. I wasn't caring about winning because of what it meant to my ego. I just wanted to win.

It was very freeing. It was for me, fundamentally, about giving up pretensions. I'm more capable now as a result of how I grew from that experience.

For example, I had had an ambition of getting a rating of 2,600, which would mean being recognized by my peers as being among the very best in the world. And I was *this close*—I had a ranking of 2,595, which was as close as you can get to 2,600 without getting it. I had that ranking for a year and a half. But I never got to where I had said I wanted to get. Never.

On the other hand, I achieved many things I never had as goals. I never had the goal to be U.S. Chess Champion, and I was U.S. Chess Champion twice. And do you know what's funny? It turns out that in the outside world, no one gives a damn whether I got the 2,600 rating or not, but being U.S. Chess Champion has opened many doors for me.

I believe that if you try to over-control what you think you will achieve, you'll miss what you can actually accomplish. I'm the kind of person who thinks I can control my destiny to a great degree, but I recognize that's not all there is to it.

I think that you should plan. I think you should be rational. I believe all that. But I also think you have to allow yourself to be free to flow with what comes up in life. You have to allow yourself to see what happens rather than have a preconceived notion of what success is going to be—what the opportunities are going to be. That is the only way to truly be the best that you can be.

—Patrick Wolff, author of *The Complete Idiot's Guide to Chess*

Dear God, I give all my dreams, my goals, and my ambitions to you. Please help my life to unfold in the Divine way that is your will. Help me not to resist, but to be aware of and to act on the opportunities presented to me. Amen

Somebody Up There Loves Me

COMMAND BY INSTINCT IS SWIFTER, SUBTLER, DEEPER,
MORE ACCURATE, MORE IN TOUCH WITH REALITY THAN
COMMAND BY CONSCIOUS MIND. THE DISCOVERY TAKES
ONE'S BREATH AWAY.
—*MICHAEL NOVAK*

I STOOD KNEE-DEEP in the snow, teeth chattering with the cold, thinking, "This is a fool's errand and I'm the fool." I'd driven about 10 miles outside of town to Sawmill Pond, a recreational area that is primarily used in the summer as a place for small children to go fishing.

The pond itself is quite large, more along the lines of a small lake. It's surrounded by acres of forest with majestic pine trees and hills sprinkled with hiking trails, all at the time buried under several feet of snow. I hadn't been to this spot in more than a decade, but I remembered having spent some pleasant afternoons here in summers long past.

I'd recently moved back to Lake Tahoe, leaving behind a stressful job as a resident hotel manager in downtown San Francisco. Ten years of a 24-hours/7-days-a-week job had taken its toll. When you live and work in the same building, there is no escape from the continual demands of the job. With the residential and the transient guests, the employees, and the maintenance requirements of the building itself, there was always someone or something needing attention. I had no personal life, no sense of privacy, and no time for myself.

I felt like I'd just been treading water for the past 10 years in an effort not to drown under the constant pressure. I wanted more than that. I wanted more than mere survival. I wanted to feel the presence of God in my life—to be aware of and able to appreciate the richness and beauty of the natural world. One of the things I hoped to accomplish by returning to a more rural environment and slower pace of life was the opportunity to reconnect with myself spiritually.

It was mid-February and still very much winter in the Sierras. My ostensible purpose in going to Sawmill Pond was to take my small dogs for an outing. I knew the area was seldom used in winter, and the parking lot plowed infrequently. I was concerned that the snow would be too deep for them to maneuver in with their short Lhasa Apso and Terrier legs. Nevertheless, I felt compelled to go.

My doubts were confirmed when I arrived at the entrance to the recreational area. I found the parking lot to be a challenge, even to my four-wheel drive vehicle. There were no other people around and the place was deserted. The snow was too deep for my dogs to navigate, except for a small area under a group of trees where it had melted. Coming here has been a waste of time, I thought. Perhaps it would be better to postpone my reacquaintance with Mother Nature until spring.

Since I had come this far, though, I decided to walk over a small rise and at least have a look at the pond. I trudged through the snow, leaving the dogs behind in the warm shelter of the car.

As I looked down at the pond, my mouth fell open in amazement. The pond had frozen over, and someone had carved a message in the snow on the surface of the pond. Written there, in gigantic letters, were the words "I LOVE GINA."

My name is Gina.

It had snowed several inches the night before. The declaration had to have been written just that morning, or it would have been obscured by snow.

As it turned out, it snowed several more inches that same night. Had I been there on any other day, the words would not have been visible, and I would never have seen them at all.

The more I thought about the extreme unlikelihood of my being at that particular place on that particular day, the more impressed I was with the magical way these seemingly random events came together. If I had ignored the compelling urge to visit this remote location, I would have missed the uplifting words that soothed my weary soul. By following my intuition, I opened a window of communication with the Divine.

I will probably never know who wrote those words, or for whom they were intended, and they will never know the impact their words had on a complete stranger. I like to think of those words in the snow as a message from God, a confirmation of the mysterious ways in which spirit moves, and that "somebody up there loves me."

—Gina Romsdahl

When we trust and follow our intuition, who knows what wonderful surprises we will discover!

Letting God Lead

GOD PULLS AND THE DEVIL PUSHES.

—STEVE MCREE

MY LIFE CHANGED FOREVER one day when my new boss called me into his office for a little talk.

At the time, a little over a decade ago, I was a successful computer systems professional, traveling first class, staying in luxury hotels, and living in a big house in Atlanta with a swimming pool—a perfect life, at least on the surface.

I had been working in the software business for years, and I had a reputation for my honesty with the customers—even when the truth wasn't the rosy picture the salespeople wanted them to hear. Sometimes my honesty got me into trouble, but we had never lost a sale because of my candor, and the customers respected and trusted me. But the new VP of sales had a different philosophy than mine. When he called me into his office that day, he told me I'd have to change two things about myself if I wanted to work for him: I'd have to forget about the Golden Rule, and I'd have to learn to lie. At first, I thought he was kidding, but it was no joke. That's when I knew I had to quit.

I started reevaluating what I wanted to do. I needed to get away and be with God, so my wife and I rented a cabin and prayed. I spent an entire night wrestling with God. My wife, Carla, said it was pretty physical—I was thrashing all around and yelling in my sleep.

At the time, I had seven job offers. The next morning, I went to a pay phone and turned down every single job. I told my wife I didn't know exactly what I was going to do, but I was going into the ministry.

Despite my training as an engineer and my experience with computers, I felt that God wanted me to work with people. So, I said, "God, here I am," and he opened the door to a children's treatment center in Knoxville, Tennessee, where my wife and I had served on the board. It wasn't at all what I had in mind. I liked kids but I had never felt very comfortable dealing with them and had no desire to work with them. But God had different plans.

So we moved to Knoxville, began a group home, and worked as administrators in the program. The changes I went through just about killed me. I went from traveling a lot and having lots of money to having little money and no vacation. We only got two nights a month off from work, and then we had to leave home and find someplace else to go, since work and home were the same place. It was a lot of dying of self. We had to relinquish a lot of what we thought we wanted to what God wanted us to do.

In four years, just when we were starting to get the hang of it, God gave me another message. One day, I was coming home from work, and I was going to a worship meeting, and God spoke to me. He told me he wanted me to write. I heard those words, but I was in a rush to get to this meeting, so I ignored them. I changed clothes, rushed down the stairs, and I heard it again. I got in the car, and just as I was about to back out of the garage, the Lord said kind of softly, "Will you go write?"

I was angry. I turned off the car, stormed inside, sat down, pulled out some paper and a pen and shouted, "What do you want?"

All he said was, "The time to resign is at hand."

On Monday, I resigned. The message from God was so clear that I thought that this period was going to be a real spiritual high, but it was the most miserable time of my life. People ruin their lives by doing what I did, but I still felt like I was doing the right thing. The Lord told me not to look for work, but to spend the time getting to know him more and letting him have more of me. I didn't know what that meant, but I thought, Okay, a couple of weeks, I can handle that.

So I was doing this, and all the while my friends were trying to get me a job. Two and a half months passed. Then my wife's parents visited. Her dad's a retired Air Force colonel, and he didn't think too much about the way his son-in-law was supporting (or not supporting) his daughter.

It was hard on me, too. I've been working since I had my first paper route at the age of ten. I started working full-time when I was fifteen, and had a 40-hour-a-week job ever since—even when I was in college.

So, I was not accustomed to not working. It didn't make sense to me. I didn't feel anything spiritual at the time, I just felt stupid. But I didn't know what else to do. I felt I was trapped, like I had no choice but to keep trusting.

Then one day, the Lord told me to go to Cades Cove in the Smokey Mountains, and he would meet me there. It was winter, raining and cold. I got there and built a little fire. I took some oats, and I thought if I got really bored, I could feed some animals or something. I sat there for five hours and didn't hear a thing. I thought, This is ridiculous.

Some birds came up in the tree I was sitting under and I thought, Okay Lord, if I really should be sitting here, have these birds eat the oats. Then I threw the oats out, and the birds just flew away. There was nothing I could make happen.

I was just sitting there with my journal and my Bible, feeling like an idiot, and just about to get up, when a deer and a fawn came out of the woods. They were 20 to 30 feet away, and they just stood there and looked at me.

I thought that was really weird. First of all, there shouldn't be a baby deer—they're born in the spring. The deer just stood there for the longest time and finally the words just started coming to me. God said, "As I provide for the deer in the woods, I'll care for you, my son." I wrote six pages, which has brought me to where I am today.

God led my wife and me to a job at Shepherd's Gate, a homeless shelter in Livermore, California. When we came out here for the interview, I told God I did not want to live in California. When I stepped inside the door of the shelter, I shouted, "Oh, no!" because I was getting a message from God that this is where he wanted us to be. Imagine going for an interview and the first words out of your mouth are, "Oh, no!" Still, I got the job.

The shelter had one small building to house women and children temporarily, but the board had ambitions to build several more facilities for longer-term residency, job training, and day care. When I started, I didn't have much experience in fundraising, and I didn't know anything about construction. I couldn't build a doghouse. But, again, God spoke to me, "If you will minister to those I send to you, I'll raise the money and I'll build the buildings," so that was our deal.

I joke about this, but it's true. I have asked three, maybe four people for money over the years, and they all turned me down. Yet we routinely get $25,000, $50,000, $100,000 in unsolicited gifts. Every time I try to raise money, I can't do it, but when I stop trying and trust, the money just comes.

Now we have expanded from our initial small shelter to a forty-bed resident's hall, an administration building, several transitional cottages, and we're still building. We never have the money when construction starts. We just have faith in God.

In October 1998, we had $130,000 in construction bills due in ten days and payroll for fifteen people due in five days, but we only had $243 in the bank. I called an executive board meeting, and they weren't real happy. I was hoping they'd fire me and get me out of this mess. I prayed to the Lord and I said, "Lord, you told me to keep building, and we kept building. What do you want me to tell them now?"

He said, "Tell them to keep building," so we kept building. Some of the board members were skeptical, but one leader said, "This is a faith walk. We just need to trust."

So, the board gave me two weeks to fix the situation, but I didn't know how to fix it. We were praying, and we sent out our normal direct mail appeal.

Suddenly we started getting 600 to 800 donations a day, six days a week. In eight weeks, $1.1 million came in. We got 7,000 new donors. Four thousand were from the appeal we sent out. The other 3,000—I have no idea where they came from.

That's the way we always do things. I don't tell the building committee how much money we have anymore; God has always provided. We have never been late one time on one single bill— never.

Carla and I thought we'd have to quit traveling when we entered the ministry, but we have traveled to some incredible places in the course of our work. Our passion is to help people who are poor, and it's taken us to places like Haiti, Guatemala, Belize, and Israel —all over the world.

The facilities here are a real miracle. We don't take any government money, and we have been able to build a campus worth more than $5 million—all paid for in cash. Since we've been here, the annual budget of the shelter has gone from $343,000 to $4 million.

I think God breathed and Carla and I have nothing to do with it—we are just here, trying to be faithful to his plan. I believe we can all hear God when we listen. Shepherd's Gate is beginning to expand into other cities. I don't know exactly where it's going, and I've learned not to tell God what I don't want to do.

Except, sometimes I mention that I absolutely don't want to retire in a big house in Maine on the ocean.

—Steve D. McRee

I trust that God has the perfect plan for my life. I don't need to figure it all out in advance. I merely need to listen for Divine guidance and have the faith to follow it.

Dreams Can Come True

IF YOU CAN DREAM IT, YOU CAN DO IT.

—*WALT DISNEY*

M Y MOTHER HAS TOLD ME that from the moment I could talk, I was a storyteller. Every night, she'd come into my bedroom, rustling around, and I'd hush her, "Shhh, I'm telling myself a bedtime story."

When I learned to write I began recording my stories on notebooks, illustrating them in rainbow Crayola colors and self-editing them along the spiral-bound margins. At age thirteen, I spent my hard-earned baby-sitting money to buy a battered old manual typewriter, and I taught myself the ten-finger system. I knew I was going to be a writer someday.

Some of the first stories I wrote on that typewriter—a collection of children's tales—were published as a book several years later. My dream was coming true.

Over the next several years, however, my dreams of writing were sidelined by the demands of real life. I got married, had children, got divorced and remarried, and had another baby. Every time I decided to take up writing again, something came up that threw me back, but I never forgot my dreams.

When our family finally bought a used computer, I discovered the Internet and the magnitude of publishing opportunities of the Web. I began to write essays about my experiences with children, womanhood, and my awakening spirituality. I gave my words freely, publishing without pay all over the Net. Occasionally, I'd get a small paycheck in the mail, but what pleased me most was the feedback from my readers.

So I was happily writing, and achieving a limited amount of success, when on the last Sunday of the year my church had a "burning bowl" service. We wrote down all the negative aspects in our lives, and then symbolically released them by burning the paper. I felt lighter as I watched my troubles and my fears go up in smoke, disintegrating as I willingly let them go—physically and psychically.

During the next part of the service, we wrote a letter to ourselves and to God, expressing the dreams and goals we wished to fulfill in the coming year. The letters were then sealed and handed over to a prayer ministry group. Just as I surrendered my problems, I let go of my ambitions, putting my intentions into form, and then sealing them away from my meddlesome control.

One of my dreams I recorded was to be able to replace my current job with paid writing jobs.

When I came home and checked my e-mail, I couldn't believe how quickly God had responded! I got an instant universal reply.

A few days earlier I'd sent a comment to a small local community paper. At the bottom of my e-mails, I always list my personal website. The editor clicked on my website, read my articles, and replied with a job offer! An offer for a job for which I hadn't applied to anyone but the Universe!

While he wasn't able to pay me a lot, it mattered that someone was actually willing to pay me at all on a regular basis. My first assignment was to get a free massage and write about it. I could never have imagined a more wonderful way to earn my first paycheck.

Later, when my daughter and her friend won top honors in an academic competition, my editor agreed to let me write an article about them, even though he couldn't pay me for it. The girls had qualified to go to the nationals several states away, but neither of our families had the money to get the girls there and pay for the hefty registration fee. One week after the article appeared, an investment banking company called. They volunteered to donate both girls' registration fee, a total of $800!

Today—nine months later—I'm getting a steady flow of paychecks for my writing. Not enough to pay all the bills yet, but the appetizers on the smorgasbord of written assignments are getting bigger and bigger. I did quit my other "day job" to focus on writing full-time. Having people recognize my name and compliment me on my articles gives me great pleasure, more than the money does.

I'm writing for the love of it, working from my heart, and having faith my dreams are just beginning to come true.

—Heide Kaminski

When we work at something we love with a joyful heart and a grateful attitude, the Universe opens wide to make way for our success.

Going with the Flow of Pregnancy

ANYTHING IN LIFE THAT WE DON'T ACCEPT WILL SIMPLY MAKE
TROUBLE FOR US UNTIL WE MAKE PEACE WITH IT.
—*SHAKTI GAWAIN*

SINCE PUBERTY, I have diligently followed the dictums of conventional wisdom and societal norms. I have attempted to starve, squish, batter, punish, and otherwise thwart my body into denying its natural tendencies, abandoning its original peaks and valleys, and streamlining itself into a long, slow curve.

But seemingly overnight, "conventional wisdom" in all its fickleness turned against me. Despite a decade and a half of conditioning to the contrary, I was ordered abruptly to reverse my ideals and embrace pounds, calories, and even fat with open arms. I was counseled to abandon my AbBlaster, dump my NutraSweet-laced diet cola down the drain, and eat steak to my heart's content.

Why did I receive this directive to let the unholy trinity of fat, sugar, and red meat cross my lips? It's simple: I was pregnant.

Being pregnant was difficult for a body-conscious female like me. My rational mind accepted that I needed to gain weight to assure a healthy baby. But my emotional side completely rejected the concept that I had to gain weight—and lots of it—to make sure that my child was healthy.

I'd spent the last fifteen years of my life fighting my body. In high school, I would live on popcorn and Diet Coke for days to shed a few pounds. In college, I ate salads and not much else for four years, showing up for daily aerobics workouts, regardless of how tired I was or how many hours of homework awaited me. I wasn't overweight, or so said the doctor's charts. But my own brain compared my reality to the pages of fashion magazines and found my body to be severely lacking.

This false—and unappreciative—body image dogged me all through my twenties. I knew it was there, but like an unwanted memory, I shoved it to the back of my consciousness, figuring that it wasn't a big deal. It wasn't until I became pregnant that I was forced to confront my issues of body image and weight head-on.

As soon as I found out I was pregnant, I decided exactly how much weight I would allow myself to gain over the course of the pregnancy—25 pounds, at the low end of the recommended range. I figured my small frame (I'm 5'4") would mean I'd gain less. I started wearing maternity clothes as soon as possible, wanting people to know I was pregnant and not "fat." I was appalled when I grew quickly, and ended up gaining my 25 pounds in the first few months.

There was more than one occasion when I'd cry after leaving the doctor's office, prompting my husband to comfort me. "Do you know how wonderful this is? Do you know what an amazing thing you are doing?" he'd remind me, telling me I'd never looked more beautiful.

Through his encouragement, I slowly began to realize what a miraculous process my underappreciated body was involved in. The pictures and information I garnered from pregnancy books helped me understand how important each and every stage of development was to my child. I wanted to give him—we knew we were having a son—the best start possible. I wasn't going to hinder his physical or emotional well-being by cutting calories or short-changing my nutritional intake. (I later discovered that research indicates that food cravings and aversions show moms-to-be what their bodies need. I knew there had to be a good reason I sent my husband out for those 3 A.M. cherry Slurpee runs!)

So as my body intuitively followed Mother Nature's plans for it, I began to relax and come to terms with my blossoming body. I knew I was healthy, and I gradually accepted that health was more important than some arbitrary notion of what I thought I *should* look like. My doctor and midwife didn't blink at my 60-pound weight gain, and my husband was complimentary until the very end—even when I outgrew my maternity clothes in my eighth month and had to buy more.

There were a host of celebrities pregnant and giving birth around the same time I was—Heather Locklear, Hunter Tylo, and Pamela Anderson Lee, to name a few—and I was less than thrilled to see how slim they looked throughout their entire pregnancies. Maybe Heather, Hunter, and Pam are genetically blessed. But a lot of the women on television, in movies, and in fashion magazines deny their bodies' wisdom and force themselves to an unrealistic standard, oftentimes risking their health. Those risks are compounded by the knowledge that while pregnant, you have responsibility not just for yourself, but for your child as well. When I see my own darling little boy, I know I did the right thing by him, and I have peace in that knowledge—even if it's peace with a few extra pounds attached.

I can't say that all my issues about my body disappeared in that short time. After all, I'd been thinking a certain way for decades. After my son, Benjamin, was born (weighing a healthy 8½ pounds), I wasn't happy to find that the pregnancy weight didn't drop off as promised by the lactation consultant and midwife. Still, a year and a half after his birth, I don't fit into the clothes I wore before I became a mommy. Even so, I've been able to set aside my strict definition of "beauty," and allow a new, broader (no pun intended!) image to emerge. I've accepted the fact that becoming a mother means surrendering your body, not just for nine months, but perhaps much longer.

I've let go of my focus on perfection, and, as a result, I'm a lot more relaxed and pleased with myself. My priorities are different; I'm more concerned about staying healthy so I can keep up with my toddler rather than fitting into a particular size or weighing an arbitrary amount. Yes, I still battle the old demons when I see superstars who are back in bikinis the week after giving birth. I probably always will.

I've learned to remind myself, though, that I need to look at my body not with an eye to how slim and trim I am, but for its strength and for what I can accomplish. Just knowing that I have the capability to sustain a life and bring a new human into the world makes me—and any woman—beautiful.

—Lain Chroust Ehmann

Going with the flow might not look like what we expect. When we let go of our preconceived ideas about how things should be—the tyranny of our minds—we can relax into acceptance and enjoy the perfect flow of life.

Hit on the Head

MY ONLY REAL COMPLAINT ABOUT GOD IS THAT I DON'T GET DIRECT MESSAGES IN MY E-MAIL THAT SAY, "OKAY, THIS IS WHAT WE'RE DOING NOW." I'D LIKE THAT CONNECTION.
—*DIANNE DEMINK*

TRAGEDY BRINGS US to our knees quickly. You get hit over the head with a baseball bat, and all of a sudden you realize you're not in control. That moment came for me when I was diagnosed with a brain tumor.

God had been throwing curve balls my way for a long time, but the brain tumor was the final strike. The pitches started coming when I was working as a food service supervisor in a nursing home in New Hampshire. An out-of-state corporation had recently purchased the home, and they were hostile to the existing management.

I'd been there nearly seven years and I'd always received excellent performance evaluations, but now I was continually criticized. Every time I saw another brown-jacketed For-Your-Eyes-Only memo in my inbox, my stomach began to contract and my heart thudded.

I prepared myself for a siege. It never occurred to me to give up, even as the harassment mounted.

Every day there were new accusations, meetings, denials of vacation and other requests. I was asked for reports no one else had to do, to work shifts no one else was required to work. I'd had diabetes since I was fourteen, but it got worse with the increased stress of the job. I saw a number of doctors, took prescription drugs for anxiety and depression, worked with a massage therapist, and hung on for six long months before they finally asked me to leave.

After losing the job, I moved to Virginia for warmer weather and a fresh start. For the first time in my life, I could not find work. I'd taught culinary arts at the college level for years, had a master's degree in nutrition, and had studied cooking in Paris, but I couldn't even get a job flipping burgers at McDonald's.

I might have reflected on that at the time, but I didn't. Instead, I worked even harder at sending out résumés, going on interviews, even putting up signs in marketplaces to hire myself out for day labor. Still nothing.

I cut my expenses by moving in with someone I had just met who was in a similar predicament. I found out she was severely mentally disturbed when I saw the writing on the wall—literally. One morning I awoke to cryptic messages written on the sides of the living room in red ink. She'd ripped the phone from its cord and she was urinating on the bathroom floor.

I escaped to live in my car with my cat.

With my belongings in storage, I drove out for a visit with my mother in Arkansas. I needed the TLC, and I got it too, but not in the way I'd imagined.

In Cooksville, Tennessee, I became so violently ill, I checked into a motel room at ten in the morning. I called Mom, explaining I was stuck at the Super-8 until I felt better. I was so dizzy I couldn't walk, my head ached, and I vomited incessantly. It turned out that the insulin pump for my diabetes had become disconnected. The ambulance rushed me to the ER not a moment too soon.

I was in diabetic ketoacidosis. This leads to coma, possibly death, if not corrected immediately. In the hospital, they stopped my vomiting, stabilized my blood sugar, and released me, wobbly and numb, after four days.

Mom urged me to visit my physician for more tests. That's when they found the brain tumor and told me that I needed immediate surgery. Somewhere in this deluge of "bad luck," I started laughing. As I hopped from one precipice to the next, it was obvious to me that fate was trying to tell me something. But I still didn't know what.

The operation for the tumor was considered a success. The cancer was gone, but I ended up in a wheelchair, unable to care for myself.

It was then that I stopped fighting. I was tired and out of options—out of work, out of money, homeless, and sick. I gave up and my life started over. I had no idea why God was pushing me in another direction; I just knew I no longer wanted to buck it. I was going with the flow. When I got out of my own way, God stepped in. He had a plan, and I was clueless.

When Mom asked me to move to her home in Arkansas, I consented without a whimper. A friend sold all of my possessions so I would have money to meet medical expenses. Fifty years worth of stuff—gone in one day.

I had nothing left except God and those he worked through. I was destitute, but I was okay. I'd stopped worrying.

Now I'm living in Hot Springs, Arkansas, this small city known for healing, surrounded by natural beauty. My life is gaining daily in the kind of solidity I've always wanted—even though God dragged me here kicking and screaming.

A lot of the things I've always wanted on an inner level, I now have. I have the time to study for a career in writing. I have the time to be with my mother. I can spend an hour and a half in the morning reading, praying, meditating, and then go to the gym for my workout.

All these desires were so much a part of me I couldn't see them. They were so close they were invisible to me. But God knew. I had been so absorbed in my own pain that I might as well have been blind.

In Arkansas my health has continually improved, and a long-desired writing career has sprouted buds. I own a small cooking business, allowing me to choose the number of hours I wish to work, so I can pursue other interests I've long neglected.

Blessing upon blessing has fallen into my life, like plums from the sky—sweet and juicy opportunities, harvested fruits of my entire life, and in an atmosphere of serenity.

I was used to making things happen, but I paid a high price for it. I always had choice and power, but that didn't mean I couldn't and didn't make stupid decisions.

There's rarely a perfect way to make any choice—there are always pros and cons. I needn't have fought my way to a happier self; I could've let go and coasted on my belief in Divine intelligence. That choice was there all along.

—Dianne DeMink

I've heard it said that we can learn through joy or learn through pain. When things are going okay, most of us aren't too motivated to stretch ourselves. It's when we're in trouble that we begin to become more receptive to lessons—if we're smart.

How many times have we felt like we knew what the right path was, but we didn't want to make the effort to change or we were scared of the risk, so we ignored our intuition? And how many times did we end up on that same path eventually—after lots of struggle? There is no avoiding some pain in life, but sometimes, the choice is ours whether to learn through joy or learn through pain.

Zen and the Art of a Bad Day

FROM A WITHERED TREE, A FLOWER BLOOMS.
—*THE SHŌYŌ RŌKU*

A FEW DAYS AGO I had a car wreck, got a bladder infection, bounced a check, locked myself out of the house, and my computer crashed. All sarcasm aside, it was a great day.

I used to think I had the worst luck in the world. Bad things seemed to happen to me all the time. I've been involved in multiple car accidents; my ceiling once caved in; my house caught fire twice; I fell off a cliff; I was mugged.

My bad luck was so common, it became part of my identity, as if I was living in a perpetual black comedy. When I'd call friends, their first question was, "Nothing bad happened to you today, did it?"

I'd laugh about it on the surface, but inside I was suffering and wondering, "Why me?" I walked around asking the Universe, "What next?!" What a mistake that was. The Universe always answered!

I felt deep despair, as if I were being tested over and over. People used to tell me, "There must be something very special in store for you." I laughed hopefully. Part of me believed there was no rhyme or reason to any of it. It was just bad luck. Part of me felt like I deserved all those bad things and was being punished for some unknown crime.

A deeper part of me wanted desperately for there to be a purpose to it all—some grand prize at the end of the line if I "passed" the suffering test.

As time went on, I began to feel very fragile, almost like I was losing my sanity. A friend told me not to worry. "When things get so bad that you cannot take it anymore, you won't break down," she said. "You'll break open." I didn't quite understand what she meant, but I hoped she was right.

One day, something in me shifted and my luck began to improve. Life seemed to stabilize. When confronted with frustrating events, I felt less affected—things just rolled off my back. I laughed with confidence, not nervousness. What had changed? Had I passed the test? Had I finally broken open?

What changed was the way I approached life's challenges. I began to realize that I had attracted every single event in my life for a reason. There wasn't good or bad luck; there was just life. I wasn't being punished; I was living a dynamic, exciting life that presented opportunities for growth at every turn.

> YOU CANNOT PREVENT THE BIRDS OF SORROW FROM FLYING OVER YOUR HEAD, BUT YOU CAN PREVENT THEM FROM BUILDING NESTS IN YOUR HAIR.
> —CHINESE PROVERB

An ordinary trip to the post office became a spiritual journey. Instead of fretting that every time I mailed a letter I got the same irritating clerk, I saw an opportunity to heal those feelings. While waiting in line, I visualized myself hugging the clerk with unconditional love. Once I looked at those feelings and accepted the circumstances, life stopped dealing me that card.

My "bad luck" became a source of spiritual growth for me. Instead of getting angry when things didn't go my way, I'd step back and think, "Why has this opportunity presented itself to me? Do I want to go through this again? What do I need to learn from this so I can move on?"

Don't get me wrong. I still don't relish the idea of life's challenges. It often takes me dozens of attempts before I understand something. But I've learned that life is full of provocations, and if I can learn to channel those moments into positive opportunities for growth, I will reap the rewards tenfold.

My car collision turned into a chance to have my air-conditioning fixed; my bladder infection was a false alarm, but I got a day off of work anyway; my computer crashing gave me a much needed break from my desk; being locked out of the house meant an hour

of birdwatching and tending my flowers; and my bounced check
. . . well, I'm still working on that one!

—Chandra Moira Beal

A Course in Miracles tells us that trials are lessons that we failed to learn, presented once again. It's up to us how we perceive a situation. We alone choose whether we learn from a problem, or whether we are destined to keep repeating the same lesson.

surrendering to love

YOUR TASK IS NOT TO SEEK FOR LOVE, BUT MERELY TO SEEK AND
FIND ALL OF THE BARRIERS WITHIN YOURSELF THAT YOU HAVE
BUILT AGAINST IT. — *A COURSE IN MIRACLES*

*I*F I EVER HAD ANY HOPE of coming across as a spiritually
enlightened being, I will completely wreck that image with
the following confession: I am a devoted fan of *Survivor*. If you've
been off on an island somewhere yourself, or you're one of those
intellectual types who doesn't own a TV, I'll explain the wildly popular television show. Sixteen people from all different age groups,
geographies, and cultural backgrounds are thrown together in some
desolate environment (the Australian outback, the African jungle, a
tropical island—you get the picture) where they compete to be the
single "Survivor," who not only wins fame, but a fortune of $1 mil-
lion. The twist is the Survivor does not win by lighting the best fires
or catching the most fish, but by managing to manipulate the rest
of the group into not voting him off. The show is morally repug-
nant, voyeuristic, often mean-spirited, and a huge ratings success.
It's also a fascinating glimpse into group psychology and social hier-
archies. But mostly it's just a guilty pleasure.

The first *Survivor* was an orgy of ego, manipulation, lies, and back-
stabbing, and the winning Survivor was the worst of the bunch. As
I watched, I wondered what would happen if a truly "light" individual, full of love and spirituality were among the group. By the third
series of *Survivor* shows, I didn't have to wonder any longer. Linda,
a self-made success and an educator from Harvard University, was
the epitome of light. She glowed authentically and relished every

moment of her experience in "Mother Africa," as she referred to her setting. When members of her own tribe (who were supposed to be working together) behaved in a nasty and petty way toward her, she quickly forgave them, and hugged each one, ready and willing to start anew, with no grudges. As she embraced the members who had wronged her, their discomfort was palpable. Her reward for her generosity of spirit? Linda was the very next person voted off.

While we can all hope that the contrived environment of *Survivor* is not representative of the real world, we must admit that the most loving, kind, and giving people are not always welcomed with open arms. Their light often reminds others of their own darkness, and it's easier for the crowd to get rid of the offending personality rather than to take the more challenging task of confronting their own demons.

It's sad to admit that love is not always the easiest or the most popular path. We're often expected to go along with the crowd, and, like the cast of *Survivor,* the crowd might not have the most loving mindset.

Remember as a kid watching the bullies on the playground, and how much easier it was to stand by and watch than to risk ourselves by defending the target of their attack? Worse yet, if we actually embraced the poor kid (an unconceivable breach of mob mentality), we would then become the new object of ridicule. Most of us didn't feel secure enough to take that kind of chance—we were just breathing a sigh of relief that we were safe for the day—so we either joined the crowd in their torment or we pretended not to notice. Expressing unconditional love in playground battles might have been the right thing to do, but I rarely saw it happen in my own neighborhood.

Now, as adults, how many times have we heard friends or neighbors gossiping about someone we know—even someone we like? How often have we spoken up for them? Too many times we're like kids back on the playground, wanting desperately to fit in at the cost of our own best impulses.

There are times when we're expected to fight, or hate, in order to fit in. Think of the Civil Rights movement in the South and how the whites who believed in equal rights were ostracized—or even killed—by those who demanded segregation.

The flames of our anger, fear, and bitterness are often eagerly fanned by "friends" cheering us on. I remember having lunch with some girlfriends and one of them lamenting to us about her mother-in-law repeatedly canceling trips to visit. Her children were disappointed when Grandma didn't show up for their birthdays or Christmas as promised, and she didn't know what to do. One friend didn't hesitate to advise, "Well, if I were you, I'd never let her see the kids again!"

We're so quick to go on the offensive, and it's easy to find support for our feelings of being wronged. It's much more challenging to find the loving solution—as it was for my friend to let go of her hurt and anger and try to understand her mother-in-law's circumstances. She learned not to create expectations for her children about when they'll see Grandma, but to simply appreciate the joy that they share when they're together—however and whenever that happens.

There are times we've held back our love, out of fear of being vulnerable. Who knows how life could have turned out differently if we consistently chose love instead fear or anger?

A best-selling author, teaching a workshop about wish fulfillment, shared a personal story.

She'd been going through a long, bitter divorce, and she had created the wish to win the battle she was having with her ex-husband. Here she was, an expert who travels the country teaching ballrooms full of people about how to make their wishes come true, and this particular wish was taking a very long time to manifest. She couldn't figure out why. She came very close to her wish, but it was not exactly to-the-letter perfect as she had imagined it, so she rejected the solution.

Gradually, she came to realize that her real wish was not to win the battle with this man (who was also the father of her son) but instead, to have a loving separation.

Sometimes we are too stupid or too stubborn to see love when it's right in front of us. If there's anything in our culture that twists the notion of surrendering to love, it's fairy tales. So it's no surprise that one of my favorite movies is the anti-fairytale, *Shrek*.

In the movie, the beautiful Princess Fiona is locked away in her castle tower waiting to be rescued by her Prince Charming. Instead, she is saved by Shrek, an ogre who is by all conventional standards ugly and gross, yet he has a distinctly un-ogre-like sensitive side.

Shrek is not what Fiona expected at all, but she has a blast with him eating roasted swamp rats and kung fu-fighting off intruders. But she has a terrible secret—she turns into an ogre at night, although she denies this reality. "I'm a princess," she says, "and this is not how princesses are supposed to look." (Who hasn't felt like that?)

It turns out that a spell has been cast on Fiona making her a beautiful princess by day and an ogre at night. "Love's first kiss" is supposed to break the spell but Fiona resists the love she feels for Shrek, moving ahead instead with the love she thought she "should" feel for the Prince Charming of the story—a short, cruel, egomaniac ruler of his own "perfect kingdom."

In the end, Fiona surrenders to the love she and Shrek share. In that magic moment, she discovers that all along she was meant to be an ogre—not a beautiful princess on a pedestal in a sad, fictitious life, admired by a man who only loves her for her looks. The best line of the movie is when Shrek kisses Fiona, breaks the spell, and she turns into her true self—an ogre. "But I'm supposed to be beautiful," she says. "You are beautiful," says lovestruck Shrek. Fiona surrenders to someone who loves her for what she is instead of what he wants her to be. She accepts her true self—green skin, big ears, and all—and, as far as we know, really does live happily ever after.

All surrenders are grounded in the principle of surrendering to love. Giving into love is often the action that results from other types of surrender. We may have to let go of our anger or give up a problem before we are ready to surrender to love. The whole practice of spiritual surrender is about letting go of fear and opening our hearts up to the miracle of love that is all around us.

The Story of Ana

WHAT MAKES THIS SUCH AN EXTRAORDINARY EXPERIENCE
FOR ME IS I'VE NEVER GONE AGAINST MY OWN RATIONAL
MIND SO STRONGLY BEFORE. I'VE HAD INTUITIONS ABOUT
THINGS, BUT THEY'RE USUALLY IN ALIGNMENT WITH THINGS
I'M ALREADY PLANNING ON DOING.
—M.J. RYAN

I WAS THIRTY-NINE YEARS OLD and an emotional wreck when I heard the voice that would lead me to the most rewarding emotional experience of my life.

The man I'd been involved with for fourteen years had just told me that he didn't love me anymore and that I had to move out of our house. I was completely devastated. Not only was our relationship ending, but I was being separated from his two children from his previous marriage, whom I had helped raise from toddlerhood. It had not always been easy or comfortable between us, and without any biological or legal ties there was no simple line of connection. I feared our relationship, too, would end.

The very first thought I had when the reality of the situation sunk in was that I should have had a child, so that I now wouldn't have to be alone.

My next thought was how crazy that was because that's not a good reason to have a child. Besides, I'd never wanted to be a mother in the first place. I'd been an "unacknowledged mother" almost my whole life—to my siblings, to my partner's children, to various friends—and I was quite resentful of the fact. These unacknowledged mother roles were very painful and ultimately unrewarding experiences. The last thing I needed to do in my life was to be a mother again.

Just as I was in the middle of this chaotic, emotional upheaval, trying to find a place to live and keep my head above water, someone told me a story about a friend of hers who had recently adopted an abandoned baby girl from China.

When I heard the story, suddenly a voice in my head said very loudly, "You're supposed to do this."

Now, I'm not a person to hear voices. I'm a very rational, practical person, and so I quickly dismissed the idea as ridiculous. "I'm an emotional wreck," I said to myself. "I'm almost forty years old, I'm alone, I've already raised two kids, which I mostly did not enjoy, and besides I have no money." So, I just brushed the voice aside and went on trying to put the pieces of my life back together.

Over the next three years, I met and married my husband. But I never forgot that voice. It never recurred, but I would often find myself drifting back to it. It had been such a strong command. What if I was supposed to listen? What would it mean to ignore such an injunction?

My husband and I started talking about having children, but I was still trying to decide with my rational mind whether or not I wanted to be a mother. Yet during this time, when I was supposedly deciding whether to have kids, there was a part of me that already knew what the outcome would be, because the voice had told me.

But I didn't allow myself to be connected on that level.

Eventually we decided we wanted children, and my husband said that he wanted to try to have a biological child. By then I had surrendered to the voice and knew what would ultimately happen. But I agreed to go along with his request. We tried for six months. One day he turned to me and said, "Maybe there's something to that voice."

The overseas adoption process takes a long, long time: Six months to do the paperwork and then a year of waiting. After our paperwork had gone to China, I was walking with my husband one evening and said, "What do you think we should name our daughter?"

As soon as I said those words, the name, Ana Li, came into my mind. It came out of nowhere. I had all kinds of ideas for names I liked, but this was the one that was given to me. We both really liked it—it was a wonderful name.

Social workers suggest that you wait until you find out what the baby's Chinese name is before you officially name her. Sometimes when they're abandoned, they have the name that the parents gave them, but usually it's the name that the orphanage workers give them. Nonetheless, it's part of their heritage, so they encourage you to try to incorporate it somehow because these babies come with so little of their past. So we decided to wait until we saw what her Chinese name was before settling on her name.

Finally we got the phone call that our baby had been assigned, and a paper came across the fax with her name and picture. Her Chinese name was Li An. The most amazing thing about this is that in China you put the last name first and the first name last. I knew this was the confirming message that I was supposed to be this person's mother. The message I had received had just turned it around the Western way.

We were warned that the babies would be small for their age and developmentally delayed because they are often left lying in orphanage cribs for months. However, we had paid for our child to be fostered (given special care), so we were not prepared for the shape Ana was in. She was particularly neglected and delayed. You could tell because she had second-degree burns from lying in urine. When I took off her diaper, skin was just hanging off of her bottom from the burns.

At thirteen months, she could not roll over. She had all kinds of autistic behaviors. She would scratch the sheets, rock compulsively, and she had no affect. The belief that this was the child I was destined to mother helped me get through my initial fears about her development.

I thought, "What this child needs is some mirroring. She needs to know there is someone with her in her world." Everyone else in our adoption group immediately put their babies in a crib to sleep. I put her on my stomach. I thought, "She's had too much crib." (In fact, she never did go in a crib again; she would stiffen and shriek at the sight of one.) While we were in China, I stayed with her in bed for two or three days. She would rock, I would rock, she would scratch, I would scratch. But she made no connection, no eye contact—nothing.

Then, one day, it was as if a light bulb came on that there was someone with her. She looked me dead in the eyes and smiled.

And then I knew everything was going to be fine.

Ana is now five years old, and she is a pure joy. She is beautiful, smart, kind, sweet. Mothering her is my consummate pleasure; she is an angel who has come into my life. Every so often, I get the sense that our coming together was destiny, the fulfillment of which I do not yet understand but that I am open to perceiving in the rightness of time.

A few days ago, we were in the car and she asked me, "Why did you go to China to get me?"

I knew the answer. "Because before you were born, your spirit came and told me that I was supposed to be your mother."

—M.J. Ryan

Some of the most amazing experiences of life open up for us when we ignore the directives of our logical, limited mind and take a leap into the love that our heart commands.

Beyond Hope

WHEN HOPE IS GONE, THERE IS STILL LOVE.

WHEN THE NURSE whispered those words to me, they didn't register. At the time I still had hope, even though my ten-year-old daughter Diana was in a situation that was anything but hopeful.

Surgery had been partially successful; it had excised a large part of the cancer that was growing in her brain. Yet the surgeon, a talented and caring man, had been stymied by his healing oath to "do no harm." Removing the entire tumor would have taken too much healthy tissue and left her incapacitated. Radiation had briefly stopped the growth of what remained, but then the dark mass reawakened and continued its inexorable spread. Standard chemotherapy drugs could not reach the foe, defeated by the barrier that the human organism has evolved to isolate the brain's blood from the rest of the body.

Now we were into our third round of experimental chemotherapy, desperately searching for something, anything, that would arrest this horrible process, somehow heal my daughter, my family, and me, and return us to a normal—now impossible—life.

This kind and compassionate nurse, administering Diana's next dose of what would prove to be another ineffective drug, could see the despair in my eyes. She had seen it before in the faces of other fathers who had brought their daughters and sons to her in their desperate attempts to keep them alive. And she offered her own piece of wisdom to me that bleak autumn morning.

Throughout most of the year and a half of Diana's ordeal, I had hope. The day that her illness was diagnosed, I was terrified but optimistic. I had every reason to hope: she was being treated in one of the top medical facilities in the world, the Lucille Packard Children's Hospital at Stanford. Her medical team was first rate:

Her surgeon was an experienced and well-regarded professor at the Stanford Medical Center, and her radiologist was the head of the department. Her pediatric oncologist was a kind and gentle man with more than twenty years of experience in the field and contacts to the latest research and pharmacological advances. If anyone could beat this thing, we could. I believed that these people could save my daughter's life. We were doing everything humanly possible, and when it came to hope I had a full measure.

Over the next year, this team went through their bag of tricks, one by one, and saw each fail. My hope began to diminish, to deflate gradually, like a child's balloon with a pinhole leak. Sometimes the news would be encouraging and the balloon would inflate again, the hope would grow almost to its original size—and then the leak would slowly empty out the hope again.

As Diana's life continued to slip away, so did my hope. It's impossible to say exactly when I realized that Diana was not going to survive. Perhaps it was during the meeting with my psychiatrist when he listened quietly to my recounting of the situation, and then told me that perhaps I should prepare myself for the worst possible outcome. Or when her oncologist told us that the latest experimental chemotherapy wasn't working—that he was running out of things to try. It could have been in one of the sessions with Diana's therapist, a remarkable woman who herself had survived brain cancer. One by one, the doctors and therapists signed off, gave out little dribbles of information in the hope that I would piece together the picture myself and relieve them of the burden of looking me in the eye and saying, "Your daughter is going to die."

But I knew. Long before anyone said it out loud, I could see it in her face. Living in a deteriorating body, experiencing the loss of function and mobility, she knew too. She told me with her eyes, those courageous and lively eyes that were her window to me, her way of reaching out to me. The surgery that was intended to save her life left her with the inability to communicate in words. Her speech worsened until she could not put together a full sentence, relying instead on gestures and expressions along with the occasional sound that she could pry loose from her failing cortex.

Those bits and pieces were more than enough to let her communicate just about anything she needed to say to me. They were enough for her to tell me that she knew she was leaving. She stopped hoping, and so did I.

But Diana never stopped living. If you have never had the privilege of being with a dying child, you cannot comprehend the level of spirit and vitality with which they respond to their circumstances. Courage is much too small and circumscribed a word to describe what goes on in a pediatric oncology ward. Behavior we call courageous to them is simply practical—the only reasonable way to approach the situation. Why contemplate the unthinkable future when today has toys and friends and *Sesame Street* and Snickers bars? Why worry about some distant, undefined fright when you have more immediate worries like yucky-tasting medicine or the dread of a needle? These blessed, valiant little warriors put us all to shame with their relentless commitment to the present moment, to life on its terms. They do more than merely cope. In some magical, mystical sense, despite their glum prognoses, as impossible as it sounds, they thrive in spirit even as their life ebbs away.

Diana thrived in spirit. Because of her growing lack of mobility, our habitual activities—tennis, swimming, bike riding—were no longer possible, so we often took long rides in the car, rides to nowhere in particular, exploring, following our noses, navigating on whim and whimsy. On one jaunt, she saw something interesting in a passing car and wanted me to understand what it was. She fumbled to form words that would not come, growing frustrated that she could not make herself clear. Finally, her face brightened. She looked straight at me, held her hands up beside her face, limp wrists mimicking a dog's paws, stuck out her tongue, and panted vigorously. "A dog! You saw a dog!" I exclaimed. She beamed, delighted that I had understood. Her speech may have been damaged, but her spirit and joy were intact.

If you've never been through this situation, you might assume that you would never give up hope. You might think that to accept that your child is dying would be an unthinkable surrender. I've been there, and I can tell you that's not the case. Human beings—

even parents—are not infinite. We cannot always control life's tragedies—even with the best surgeons and hospitals.

And we cannot continue to hope beyond hope as someone we love gradually, painfully succumbs to the effects of a fatal disease. There comes a moment when the balloon is empty, too tattered and worn to hold air any longer. There comes a time when we must stop fighting what we cannot change, and we must start accepting—cherishing the love that is present and putting all of our energies into expressing that love.

Paradoxically, when I came to this realization, I experienced an unanticipated sense of relief. Diana's battle with cancer was over, and so was my struggle with hope. I surrendered to the inevitable. With hope gone, all that remained was love. I could tend to the business at hand without distraction—enjoy the present with my daughter and give over my complete attention to caring for her immediate needs.

We arranged her dolls around her on the couch, watched cartoons together, and ate her favorite macaroni and cheese dinner night after night. I rubbed her feet to calm her, gave her baths, and tucked her in bed at night, saying, "I love you." I savored each moment with her, banked those memories against that coming day when they would be all I would have of her.

Finally, her care became too difficult to manage at home, and she went to the hospital for the last time, to die in as much comfort as possible. Diana's mother, sister, and I took turns being with her, so that she was never alone. I particularly looked forward to sleeping in her hospital room overnight, to help her go to the bathroom or comfort her after a bad dream. Toward the end, Diana lapsed into a merciful unconsciousness. She continued to hold onto life, but she was also preparing for the journey ahead. My role was simply to be present, nothing more.

Our last few days together were given over to saying good-bye, saying to her all the things that I needed to say, knowing that she heard me through the fog of her coma. I told her stories of the happy times we had had together, of volleyball games at Stanford and trips to the beach and license plate bingo and our silly word games. I let her know how much I was going to miss her and that I would take care of her sister. I sang to her, songs that I had sung throughout her lifetime, folk ballads and children's songs, church hymns and Top 40 songs and show tunes. The day she died, I sang her an Irish lullaby, kissed her on her freckled forehead, arranged the covers up under her neck just the way she liked them, and gave her over to her mother's care. The phone call that night was expected—no surprise. Diana and I had already said our good-byes. I released her now to her passage, with sadness but also with love.

In a well-known passage, Saint Paul said, "There remain faith, hope and love, these three; and the greatest of them is love." In walking a path that no parent can imagine, I have learned that he is right. At the beginning of Diana's ordeal, faith in the healing power of modern medicine buoyed me. As her health steadily failed, I clung desperately to every shred of hope, as does a sailor to his sinking ship. In the end, with nothing left to believe in, with no more hope to cling to, I was forced to surrender all and, in doing so, learned the most profound lesson of my life:

Always, beyond faith, beyond hope, always, there is still love.

—Edward Mason Morgan

May we have the strength to love when we are most hopeless, to seize the beauty of the moment, even when all we have are a few precious moments.

Auntie

AND THINK NOT YOU CAN GUIDE THE COURSE OF LOVE. FOR
LOVE, IF IT FINDS YOU WORTHY, SHALL GUIDE YOUR COURSE.
—*KAHLIL GIBRAN*

WHEN I WAS YOUNG I had this grand plan all worked out in my head of what my life was going to be like when I grew up.

I would be married by the time I was twenty-six years old and have my first child at age twenty-eight. That would give me two years before my second child was born when I was thirty. I would have it all—a loving husband, two beautiful children, and a successful career in my chosen field of work. Life would be perfect.

But it didn't happen like I had planned—none of it. By my mid-twenties I had become disillusioned and disheartened with my life. A university degree had not secured me the kind of work I wanted; I didn't even have a full-time job. Instead I was struggling to get by and pay my bills on two dead-end part-time jobs.

With relationships, things were not much better. After a string of boyfriends and one broken engagement, I was still single with no possibilities on the horizon. I was going nowhere fast—and I knew it.

Then something completely unexpected happened that changed my life. When I was twenty-seven years old, my younger sister had a baby.

I'd always envisioned myself having the first baby in our family and giving my parents their first grandchild, but instead the honor went to my sister Laurel. I can't deny that it hurt but life, as I was beginning to learn, doesn't always turn out the way we expect.

My sister had a beautiful, healthy baby girl. I loved her as if she were my own from the day she was born. They named her Cassidy Elizabeth.

I took my duties as aunt very seriously. I did whatever I could, whenever I could, to help out. When my sister ran into far too many child care problems upon returning to her job, I rearranged my work schedule so that I could take care of my niece during the three days that my sister was away from home. It required some hefty compromise on my part, but I made it work. I didn't want my niece shuffled in and out of a day care center where she would become just one of many children. I wanted her needs to be paramount, and I knew I could do a better job than a day care worker could. After all, I was family and cared more than any stranger ever would.

My niece was melting my heart and burrowing deeper into it every day, only I didn't realize it yet. But soon I would know. She was growing older and learning more all the time. I was able to be a part of her overall development, and I couldn't have been happier.

One day when Cassidy was three and a half years old, I took her to her favorite hamburger place for lunch, as I had many times before. This time was different however. Something amazing was about to take place. Sitting across from me, chewing earnestly on her french fries, she locked eyes with me and said completely spontaneously, "I wuv you Auntie."

My heart almost burst forth from my chest at the sound of those words. The look of childish happiness on her face when I told her I loved her, too, was pure magic.

The more time I spent with Cassidy the more I began to realize that my mindset was changing—for the better. I no longer was nearly as concerned about my low income, and my dead-end jobs didn't seem quite so dead anymore. In fact my priorities were no longer the same. I hadn't planned on becoming an aunt before a mother. Cassidy's birth didn't directly affect my life, yet my life was transforming because of her.

Instead of harboring hurt and disappointment, I was surrendering to the miracle of her life and rejoicing in it. I couldn't control everything, and that was okay. I could embrace all the unexpected twists and turns that life sent my way. Seeing the world through her eyes, I gained a fresh perspective on my own life. I realized that I'd shed my ideas of "grand plan" for my life and was focusing instead on all that my life was.

I was blessed with so many wonderful things, including my sweet niece. I had to concentrate on the haves of my existence, not the have nots.

I'm still waiting for some of the pieces to fall into place in my life, but I no longer despair about things I can do nothing about. I am where I am supposed to be, doing what I am supposed to be doing. As far as I'm concerned, that's good enough for me.

—Anika Logan

Life doesn't always work exactly as we planned. Love can show up in a package that's quite different than the one we expected. Grab it anyway! Enjoy the wonder of love no matter how it materializes.

Angel Action

LET A MAN OVERCOME ANGER BY KINDNESS, EVIL BY GOOD.

NEVER IN THE WORLD DOES HATRED CEASE BY HATRED;

HATRED CEASES BY LOVE.

—*BUDDHA*

O N A COOL FALL NIGHT in Wyoming in 1998, Matthew Shepard, a twenty-one-year-old, 5'2", 105-pound college student, was kidnapped, driven to a remote prairie, robbed, and pistol-whipped while he begged for his life. His killers—high on methamphetamines—tied him to a wooden fence, took his shoes, and left him for dead in the freezing night. Eighteen hours later a cyclist thought he saw a scarecrow hidden in the sagebrush. When he looked closer, he discovered it was Matthew—his face was covered in blood, except for the trails of his tears. Matthew died five days later.

When Matthew's family and friends gathered in Laramie, Wyoming, for his funeral, they were not alone. The national media rushed to cover the brutal murder, and sympathetic mourners traveled from all over the country. But there was also a small group who had traveled from Kansas with a different purpose—to deliver a message of rage and hatred.

Matthew was homosexual, and that was enough to make some people hate him. First, the two men who killed him, and then, a group from Westboro Baptist Church in Topeka, Kansas, led by Reverend Fred Phelps, an anti-gay activist. As Matthew's loved ones eulogized him, Phelps and his protestors stood in the rain and snow, carrying signs with pictures of Matthew proclaiming, "Matthew in Hell" and "God Hates Fags," as they chanted, "Fags die, God laughs."

When Phelps and his flock returned, months later, for the murder trial, a group of Matthew's friends decided to do something.

One might expect an ugly confrontation—hatred and rage spewing back and forth across the groups—trying to overpower each other with sheer volume and mass.

Shepard's friends had every reason to reflect Phelps' malice back to him. Fueled by grief and injustice—and with most of the town and country on their side—it would have been understandable to attack Phelps' cruel prejudice. Nobody would have blamed them; they had a right to be angry. But instead they chose a remarkable path of love.

Matthew's friends chose to take action—"Angel Action." Romaine Patterson, one of the organizers, said, "After seeing Fred Phelps protesting at Matthew's funeral and finding out that he was coming to Laramie for the trial, I decided that someone needed to stand toe-to-toe with this guy and show the differences. And I think at times like this, when we're talking about hatred as much as the nation is right now, that someone needs to show that there is a better way of dealing with that kind of hatred."

So seventeen "angels"—wearing costumes made of white bedsheets stretched across plastic pipes to make enormous wings, and gold halos on their heads—stood silently outside the county courthouse, completely blocking the Kansas protesters from view. The angels wore earplugs, so they couldn't hear Phelps' rants, and they stood with their backs to the protesters, flapping their wings in a show of solidarity and peace. Some in the crowd began singing "Amazing Grace."

Matthew's friends called their movement, "Angel Action," and their purpose, according to one organizer, "We want to send a message of love."

"I could no longer sit idly by and watch others bring forth messages that were nothing more than vindictive and hate-filled," said Patterson. "I feel it is necessary to show the great nation that we live in that there doesn't need to be this kind of violence and hatred in our world."

So the angels spread their wings and gently spread their peace.

—Kathy Cordova

Sometimes it seems as if anger and attack are the only reasonable options. Yet it is when we go beyond reason, to the heart, that we find the forces within ourselves and the strength to love.

When Lightning Strikes

A GOOD FRIEND RECENTLY ASKED ME, "EVER WORRY THAT
LIFE IS GOING ALONG TOO PERFECTLY? THAT LIGHTNING
WILL STRIKE AND SOMETHING HORRENDOUS WILL HAPPEN,
THAT CHANGES YOUR LIFE FOREVER?"

"NO," I ANSWERED HONESTLY, "I DON'T WORRY, BECAUSE
IT ALREADY HAS AND WE'RE OKAY. WE'RE DOING JUST FINE.'"
—*GRACE MINA NAVALTA*

"WHAT DO YOU WANT, a boy or a girl?" people would ask when
I was pregnant with my second child.

I knew what I was supposed to say. The laws of social grace and
unconditional motherly love deemed that I smile and say, "Oh, it
doesn't matter, as long as it's healthy." But the truth was I really
wanted a girl.

I knew how hollow that sounded, but I didn't care. I had a terrific husband, a beautiful two-year-old son, and we had just moved
into the house of our dreams. I longed for a little girl to round out
the perfect family and my ideal life.

I came from a large family where money was scarce. College
was my ticket to a better life, and I learned early on that you can
accomplish anything with a good education, hard work, and the
drive to make things happen. I had worked hard and built a successful career as a business consultant at a major Silicon Valley
company. I traveled all over the country, managing projects, and
handling whatever problems came my way.

Out-of-control situations were what happened to other people,
and I felt I'd proven that I could handle any of life's challenges.
Sometimes I even believed that I could almost will things to happen,
so when the doctor told me I was having a girl I wasn't surprised.

Although my pregnancy wasn't perfect, it was routine—nothing
that would prepare me for what happened in my eighth month,

when the "lightning bolt" struck. I was at a routine checkup when the doctor warned in a quiet, but urgent voice, "The baby is moving too slowly. You need to have an ultrasound right away."

The test revealed that the baby was barely moving. If we didn't get her out immediately, she would die.

My daughter, Arianna, was delivered breach by emergency cesarean two hours later. Only 2 pounds, 13 ounces, she was not expected to live. I was in so much pain, the doctor wanted to immediately sedate me, but I begged him to wait until I touched her tiny chest and felt her feathery soft breath. "She's alive!" I thought and drifted off into unconsciousness.

Every day I pumped my breastmilk, left my son in someone else's care, and drove 30 miles to the hospital. As I rocked Arianna and sang to her, I fell in love with her tiny face. I tried to ignore the fact that she was as limp and floppy as a rag doll. I became obsessed with waking her and getting her to suck on her own. Still, she continued to be fed by tube and could only suck from a bottle when given oxygen.

I tried to hold on to the belief that nothing was wrong. But as the days in the hospital turned into weeks, Arianna missed every important milestone. At nine weeks, she couldn't move her head; she didn't smile or respond to me. I was on a roller coaster and fluctuated between absolute certainty that she would never walk or talk, to believing that she'd be all right, a "regular kid."

"Please God," I begged. "Don't do this to me. Don't do this to my little girl. She's just a baby." I felt an ocean of sadness well up inside, as wave after wave of disappointment washed over me, changing my world forever.

As Arianna was released from the hospital, I became obsessed with finding her the perfect therapist and the best program. If I just did the right things, got her the right services, I could fix things just like I'd always done in the past. There were no tests, nothing definitive to say that there was something actually wrong with my baby, so I knew I could beat this thing—whatever it was.

But I felt that God turned his back on me when I learned Arianna was diagnosed with Prader-Willi Syndrome—a rare birth defect that causes mental retardation and a whole host of mental, physical, and behavioral problems. I was devastated. How could this happen? My whole life, I could work through any problem, overcome any barrier. But now God was handing me a life sentence.

I grieved over the child that I had expected but would never come. Small things that I hadn't even realized were important to me hurt the most. She would never be a cheerleader the way I was in high school. She would not be the popular girl I imagined, nor would she learn to drive a car or do a thousand other things normal teenagers do. Would she ever wear the beautiful ivory wedding dress that I dreamed of passing on to my daughter? I didn't know, but I did know for certain that she could never have children.

I was heartbroken but I was still going to fix things. She would be the best-educated disabled child. I read up on her birth defect—I became an expert. I learned stimulation exercises and anything else I thought would help. Because of my efforts she would lead a normal or close to normal life, I thought. But there was always a sense of frustration, helplessness, and failure. There was always a feeling that if I just tried harder, if I found the right therapist or program, I could make her better. But the perfect therapist or program was never found. I had to let go of my dreams of a perfect daughter and a perfect life.

Arianna moved forward, but always months or years behind other children her age. She spoke her first word at fifteen months. She walked at twenty-seven months. There was nothing I could do to speed her progress. Every day I prayed for a miracle.

Then, one day, after years of gradual development, the miracle happened. Arianna didn't change, but I did. One day at preschool I watched her struggle with recognizing a letter, then a number. It struck me how truly difficult it was for her to do some of the simplest things that other children and parents take for granted. It was like a light inside of me finally was turned on. This is who she is; a kid for whom nothing comes easily. This is the way she would always be. There was no point to pushing or controlling. Arianna moved at her own pace and, like a bud opening in springtime, she would bloom at her own time.

At that moment, I finally let go and accepted all of her differences and her special gifts—her open and trustful nature, her perpetually happy disposition, and her exuberant and engaging personality. I felt a sense of peace that I never had known before. Then I knew that I could accept her and enjoy her without always wanting and expecting more.

Still, the day she started kindergarten I was racked by worry and guilt. She was mainstreamed into a regular kindergarten class. "Was this the right thing to do?" I thought. Or was my own desire for her to be a "normal" kid clouding my judgment?

The kindergartners lined up, proudly bearing their new clothes and school supplies. A burst of apprehension pulsed through me as Arianna marched up into line, her hair bobbing and her bright purple backpack slung over her shoulder. I rushed up next to her and tried to lead her inside. She turned and said, "Go Mamma. Go way now." My eyes blurred with tears as I watched her walk into the classroom. I knew, against all odds, with every child there being able to think faster and understand so much more, none had more courage than Arianna—the little girl with the brave heart.

I was awestruck by her sense of purpose and the triumph of her will over her disability and at that moment I realized, through the eyes of love and acceptance, my daughter Arianna was perfect.

—Grace Mina Navalta

Sometimes in our frantic struggle to control people or situations—to make them the way we think they should be—we miss the wonder of the reality that is. Each of life's difficulties bestows a gift—if we only open our eyes and our hearts to let in the light.

The Man in the Mirror

A LOVING PERSON LIVES IN A LOVING WORLD. A HOSTILE
PERSON LIVES IN A HOSTILE WORLD: EVERYONE YOU MEET IS
YOUR MIRROR.
—KEN KEYES, JR.

WHEN I WAS SIX YEARS OLD I learned my first lesson about
recklessly expressing love. I had a crush on Jeff Knox, the boy
next door, and one dull summer day, egged on by our bored siblings, I decided to act on those feelings. I chased poor Jeff back
and forth between our yards, trying to consummate my feelings
with a kiss. A brighter girl might have surmised that his running
away and screaming for mercy meant that my affections were
unrequited but I must have just figured he was playing hard to get.
Finally Jeff's older brother captured him and held him down so I
could bestow a peck upon his cheek.

Little did I know, my father was watching this whole scene from
our kitchen window, and he called me immediately inside and told
me—in no uncertain terms—that nice little girls did not chase
boys around and try to kiss them. Mom backed him up, adding her
own philosophy of feminine wiles—that you should never chase a
boy; you should always let him chase you. I could not have been
more embarrassed. I was scorned, not only by my first love but by
my parents, too. Even though it was the '60s, my days of free love
were over. I had learned my lesson.

From that point on, the polite young lady in my head told me
that it was a breach of etiquette to be the first to demonstrate love.
My "Southern Belle" persona—groomed by my homecoming
queen mother—told me that professing love too quickly would
cause me to lose my strategic advantage in the game of romance.
Over time, I developed my own personality—the "in control" me,

who grew cautious about letting down the barbed wire that protected my heart.

So mostly I kept any loving feelings I thought might be unreciprocated to myself, like a reasonable mature adult. Within the tight perimeter of my husband, children, and parents, it was okay to say, "I love you," but love was still a preciously guarded treasure, not something to be spread around like confetti on New Year's Eve. Even telling my big, strong, bearlike father, "I love you," as we ended a phone call across 3,000 miles, felt a little like an emotional stretch.

Until I met Ira—the man in the mirror.

I was at a holistic spa in the desert—my version of heaven on earth. I had taken this trip by myself—no kids waking me up at 6 A.M. and no husband to ask, "What's for dinner?" Just the time alone was pure luxury—not to mention the gourmet food, massages, seaweed wraps, and a staff that seemed to anticipate my every need and fulfill it like a Jewish mother with ESP.

I exercised my body in all the standard-issue aerobics classes and nature hikes, but this resort wasn't just about shaping up abs and thighs. This was a mind-body-spirit spa, with a more ambitious goal than merely shedding a few extra pounds on the physical plane. This spa aimed to teach its overworked, overscheduled, overstressed clientele the art of "mindfulness."

I quickly figured out how deceptively simple the concept was. Pay attention, be present, and enjoy the moment you are in—instead of rehashing the past or fretting about the future. Not a problem here, where my present included having my body expertly kneaded by Geng, the Greek god massage therapist with the amazing hands. Here, being aware of my present was infinitely more satisfying than obsessing over my past or worrying about my future. Mindfulness was pure pleasure.

There was a steady stream of workshops on the subject—Mindful Eating, Mindful Stress Reduction, Mindful Relationships, but since I was only there for four days, I decided to get right to the point and take the Mindful Decision Making class. It was near the end of my stay, and I was relaxed to an almost vegetative state, feeling the immense peace and beauty of the desert. I had no idea what to expect of the class, but being perpetually indecisive, I figured I was bound to learn something.

The workshop was packed. About thirty people were sitting around congenially in a big circle, chatting about their latest lavender–ylang-ylang massage or the strawberry walnut spinach salad at lunch. The class varied drastically in age—from early twenties to seventies—with more men in the group than the largely female spa population would suggest.

This spa was not cheap, and this group was unquestionably affluent, sporting shiny designer spandex and unscuffed athletic shoes. They had the look and feel of people who are used to having their way in their business and personal lives. They didn't look like people who had trouble making decisions, but maybe they just had a space in their schedule to fill in between reflexology and Pilates.

The workshop began with all the participants going around the circle, introducing ourselves by first name and vocations as varied as attorneys and full-time mothers. Then we began the first exercise—a story to which we were asked to respond:

You are in love and engaged to be married. Your fiancé gives you a beautiful, very valuable engagement ring—a family heirloom that once belonged to his grandmother. Later, your future mother-in-law pulls you aside and asks you to sign a legal document requiring you to return the ring in case the marriage is dissolved. What would you do?

The cheerful veneer of the room quickly dissolved into war.

"I would give the ring back right then and I'd cancel the wedding!"

"I would not sign the contract because I wouldn't want her to think that she can control me."

"I would tell my fiancé that he had to choose between me and his mother."

And on and on. This story had definitely struck the mother-in-law Achilles' heel of a bunch of women in the group.

Then, the men (especially the lawyers) chimed in. "Well, legally speaking, if the ring belonged to the fiancé and not his mother . . ."

This class was ready for battle on all fronts—legal, material, moral, and emotional. They were so enraged I thought they were going to rustle up a lynch mob and hang the fictitious mother-in-law in effigy.

Their responses stunned and frightened me. Not because I had an heirloom ring or a son anywhere near marriageable age, but because of the intensity and immediacy of the hostility in the room. It felt like the whole crowd was a big simmering pot of repressed anger on the verge of boiling over with the slightest increase in temperature.

Now, I can get as angry as the next person. And I've been known to let myself get whipped into a manic frenzy along with the crowd, but that wasn't happening this time. Maybe my first reaction would have been similarly angry (or rational, like the lawyers) had I not been so relaxed. But instead, I experienced a rare moment of clarity. I instantly realized how quickly we think the worst of people and how easily, and how we spew our venom, forever poisoning a situation, like a cobra intent on striking first at the mere sound of a rustle in the leaves.

But I didn't share my reaction. Maybe all those aromatherapy treatments had seeped some unnatural chemicals into my brain, I thought. I was sure the class would think I was a New Age-y/space cadet/doormat if I said, "Sign the agreement. Who cares about the ring? If the marriage ends, why would you want it anyway, especially when it means so much to the mother?"

So I kept my mouth shut.

We sludged through a couple of similar exercises with close to the same results. I think were supposed to be learning to make decisions mindfully, in the present, instead of merely reacting, but the lessons didn't seem to be "taking" very well.

Finally, it was time for the last exercise of the class. We were asked to team up into pairs with someone we didn't know. The room shifted uncomfortably as people scanned the room to find a stranger who seemed like a reasonably sane enough person with whom to interact. I turned to the person to my immediate left—a thin, elderly man with wisps of gray hair surrounding his mostly bald, slightly sunburned head. His name was Ira. He gave me a shy smile and seemed relieved to find a partner without having to expend too much energy.

Next, we were asked to stare into our partner's eyes for seven minutes without talking—without interruption of any kind.

Almost no one could do it. It was too uncomfortable to stare straight into the soul of a complete stranger. Giggles erupted in the room. This group that found it so natural to voraciously spout their hostility could not look silently into another person's eyes for a few short minutes.

For some unknown reason, I found the exercise easy. Maybe because the man I partnered with had such kind, pale blue, twinkly eyes. Maybe because he didn't seem threatening to me in any way. But he couldn't keep quiet or focus on me. He looked away, looked at the floor, and made several half-hearted attempts to talk to me. I didn't say a word, just stared straight at him, smiled, and concentrated on mentally sending him thoughts of love and acceptance for the full seven minutes.

When the exercise was over and we were asked, "How did it feel?" I had a hard time actually saying what I felt. I was more than a little afraid to tell this group that I had felt great love for this stranger with the kind eyes. Would they laugh? Would they think I was some kind of weirdo? It didn't matter; my feelings were so intense, so immensely joyful, that they couldn't be contained—they just came crashing out, "I feel complete love for this man. Looking into his eyes, I felt total bliss, pure love. Ira, I love you!"

The words didn't sound like something I would ever say, but sure enough, they were coming from me—from some deep-down place inside myself that I'd never felt comfortable letting loose.

I was so enjoying my mindful feelings that the reaction of the group melted away. To this day I don't remember how they responded. But I do remember Ira's reaction. He didn't run away; he beamed.

—Kathy Cordova

Every person we encounter is a mirror for us. It's our choice what we see in that mirror. If we choose to see love, love will be reflected back into our lives.

Think of someone you don't like very much, or whom you believe doesn't like you. Imagine surrounding that person with a golden glow of love, flowing straight from your heart. The next time you see that person, try this for five minutes and watch what happens.

Surrendering to Grace

MY GRACE IS SUFFICIENT FOR YOU, FOR MY POWER IS MADE
PERFECT IN WEAKNESS."
— *2 CORINTHIANS 12:9*

THAT SUNDAY MORNING in May began like any other and held no promise of the transformation in store for me. My work at a boutique had become a form of therapy after losing the baby eight months before. Somehow being surrounded by women and clothing gave me a sense of kinship and femininity that I desperately needed. Living in a house with my husband and two small boys is wonderful, but definitely has its testosterone moments. Months earlier, we were ecstatic when we discovered I was pregnant, and when we found out the baby was a girl, I had never been happier. Her name was Grace. When we lost her, so many dreams and hopes died with her. The pain was all-encompassing.

That Sunday in the boutique it seemed lonely and quiet. There was a street fair, and I could expect very few customers to make the trip down the side street to the store.

As I walked around the boutique, I started to think about baby Grace. How I never held her, the terrible way we had lost her. How on that September morning I had gotten out of bed and prepared for my day. Barric, my five-year-old, had school and Brennon, my three-year-old, was coming along with my husband David and me on our doctor's visit. I was in my seventeenth week of pregnancy, anticipating a due date of March 3. This was the big appointment where we would find out the sex of the baby. Brennon was so excited. We had pumped him with all the wonderful things being a big brother would entail. At the doctor's office the ultrasound revealed the happy news that we were having a girl. But the joy was quickly destroyed by a despairing revelation: There was no heartbeat. David rushed Brennon out of the exam room so he wouldn't see me fall apart, somehow making it home without breaking down himself. So I sat there sobbing all alone.

When David returned, the doctor came in and told us how sorry he was that our baby was no longer alive, and that given how far along I was they would need to induce labor. I wanted to die. How could there be no heartbeat? I had two wonderful pregnancies and delivered two healthy boys. None of this seemed real, and it was so overwhelming that I could not move or think. How were we going to explain this to the boys?

Later, in the labor and delivery room, as the nurse started the IV, I could hear a woman giving birth in the next room. It was more than I could bear, and the nurse helped me to the bathroom where I vomited over and over again until I was empty. I tried to stand and collapsed into her arms. No words were spoken. No words exist that could express what was happening to me or how I was feeling. She helped me back into the hospital bed, where I lay silently praying for angels to please help me through this.

I felt like I had failed on so many levels as a woman. Why was my body—which had twice done this—unable to do it this time? As a wife and mother, I had failed everyone—especially the baby girl inside me. I tortured myself by analyzing everything I'd done, everything I'd eaten in the past month. Frantically my mind grasped for an explanation to this horror and found nothing. When the doctor returned, he told us all the tests and blood work results were normal. There simply was no medical rationale for what had happened.

As I lay there waiting for the drugs to take effect, David and I discussed names for the baby and decided on Grace Anne, after my paternal great grandmother. Soon a nurse walked in with a clipboard and in a very scripted voice outlined what we could expect. Without emotion and with great efficiency, she clinically described the delivery and ensuing details. Then she rushed out as fast as she had come in. "What a horrible job she has," I thought to myself, as nausea overcame me again. That day soon turned into the next, and baby Grace was still not delivered. The doctor decided it had been long enough, and she was taken surgically. Just like that, I was pregnant one day and not the next, and nothing to show for it except a load of hospital paperwork, a cotton ball with tape over it where my IV had been, and a gaping scar on my heart.

Telling the boys was impossibly hard. Brennon could not understand why he could not see baby Grace or hold her. He would not even look at me when I came home—as if he were affirming everything I was feeling. Barric acted like he understood, and then asked me if God would give us another baby even though I hadn't taken care of the first baby. Again, my child was expressing the very thing I was feeling. I walked away, holding back my tears until I safely reached my bedroom. There again, I prayed for angels to help us through this. The days turned into weeks and then months, and my March 3 due date came and went with only silent tears. I would cry myself to sleep every night. Brennon started preschool and seemed to love it. David was back to work, and life seemed to take on a recognizable normalcy. I started working at the boutique that fall.

Now it was spring, and I was walking around the store looking at all the clothes that had just come in for the summer season. They were all loose fitting and would make great maternity clothes, I thought to myself. Then out of my mouth, and across my lips I asked Jesus out loud to give me a sign, telling me if I was meant to have another baby. At that very moment I heard a noise at the front of the store and turned to see a young woman trying to get her stroller up the step and into the door. I quickly walked over to help her. I looked into the stroller and saw a beautiful baby girl with the largest blue eyes I had ever seen. I smiled at the baby and said, "You are the sweetest thing. What's your name?"

The mother smiled and said, "Her name is Grace Anne and she was born March second." I nearly fell to my knees. I felt all the air being sucked out of the room around me, and a wave of emotion hit me with such force I could not hold back. I began sobbing, and through my tears I somehow managed to explain to the woman how I too had a baby girl named Grace, who had died months before her due date of March 3. I also told her how, just before she came into the store, I had asked God to give me a sign if I was meant to try again. The woman looked at me as if she felt my heartbreak the way only another mother could. She scooped up baby Grace and handed her to me as she said, "I think this is your answer."

In that moment I felt all the love a mother feels for her child flow through me; all my pain and grief were leaving me, and my broken heart began its surrender to feelings of peace and hope.

As I held that baby, all my hungry senses were engaged—I was cradling, smelling, seeing, experiencing for a moment what my heart had longed for, and in doing so, I let go. Instead of emptiness, I felt the shock of fullness and the power of hope. I realized that I wanted to give up the pain and stop questioning myself and questioning God. For the first time I truly believed that I could heal. I would never be whole but I could be less broken. And I surrendered to the power of love.

In that moment I released the guilt I had been holding so tightly and took responsibility for my healing. It was not within my power to save Grace but it was within my reach to help myself and my family. Where once I had felt despair and emptiness when I closed my eyes and thought of baby Grace, I now saw a beautiful angelic face. That connection with a compassionate stranger and a precious baby gave me the courage to let go of my pain and embrace life again.

—Carrie Morris

Lord of infinite mercy, see our brokenness and gather the pieces unto You. Where we are open, where we are empty, fill us with your spirit. Cradle us in the arms of your wholeness and light our souls with hope. Soothe our hearts and gently guide us to accept your peace, seek your comfort, and surrender to your love.

The Christmas Truce:
AN OUTBREAK OF PEACE

THE ONES WHO CALL THE SHOTS WON'T BE AMONG
   THE DEAD AND LAME,
AND ON EACH END OF THE RIFLE WE'RE THE SAME.
—*SILENT NIGHT: THE REMARKABLE 1914 CHRISTMAS TRUCE*

IN DECEMBER 1914, World War I had been raging for less than five months, yet hundreds of thousands of men had been killed, wounded or reported missing during its brief course.

Along the front lines, conditions were inhuman. Latrines were nearly non-existent and accomplishing bodily functions a nightmare. It was a landscape of fortified ditches of "lice, rats, barbed wire, fleas, shells, bombs, underground caves, corpses, blood, liquor, mice, cats, artillery, filth, bullets, mortars, fire, and steel."

Christmas was approaching, a festive time common to all combatants—the British, French, and Belgians on one side and the Germans on the other.

The Pope had called for a cease-fire at Christmas, but it was quickly rebuffed by both sides as "impossible." *The New Republic* suggested sardonically, "The stench of battle should rise above the churches where they preach good-will to men. A few carols, a little incense and some tinsel will heal no wounds." A wartime Christmas would be a festival "so empty that it jeers at us."

Thus, both sides expected no letdown in the war. Separated by the miserable waste of No Man's Land as Christmas approached, troops seemed likely to enjoy nothing of the holiday's ambience— not even mere physical warmth. Cold rain had muddied and even flooded many trenches, and decomposing bodies floated to the surface.

Yet in this nightmare of war, a basic human yearning for peace bubbled up from the soldiers, often against the direct orders of their commanders. Although we know the truce began among the lower ranks, no one was certain exactly where and how it had begun.

But on Christmas Eve, 1914, the enemies laid down their arms and celebrated Christmas together in a spontaneous gesture of peace on earth and good will toward men.

One legendary story symbolizes the spirit of the truce:

In the German trenches, on Christmas Eve, a determined pastry cook from Berlin, Alred Kornitzke, was making marzipan balls, a traditional festive confection, for his company, while bullets flew around him.

"No one can do this to me," Kornitzke exploded.

Seizing a Weihnachtsbaum (a Christmas tree) as holy protection, he lifted it high and, still wearing his white baker's cap, ran toward the enemy lines. The enemies were baffled by the apparition, for the German appeared too crazy to shoot at and too comical to take seriously. They watched him in amazement; he did not stop until he was halfway between the lines. There he set the tree down carefully, calmly took some matches he had intended to use for his petroleum stove, and in the frosty, star-filled night, lit the candles one by one.

"Now, you blockheads," he shouted, "now you know what's going on! Merry Christmas!"

The enemy fire ceased. Kornitzke stumped back to his lines and to stirring his precious marzipan mixture before an audience of admiring soldiers.

Elsewhere, the truce began with shared traditions and song, as the two sides approached one another. Yuletide carols initiated a tentative courtship that developed into greetings shouted across lines, and the enemies gathering to bury their dead together. Soon the soldiers were talking and smoking together and playing impromptu soccer games. Ultimately the soldiers shared their most valued commodities—food and tobacco and souvenirs such as uniform buttons and insignia.

One British lieutenant wrote to his mother, "a most extraordinary thing happened. . . . Some Germans came out and held up their hands and began to take in some of their wounded and so we ourselves immediately got out of our trenches and began bringing in our wounded also. The Germans then beckoned to us and a lot of us went over and talked to them and they helped us to bury our dead. This lasted the whole morning and I talked to several of them and I must say they seemed extraordinarily fine men. . . . It seemed too ironical for words. There, the night before we had been having a terrific battle and the morning after, there we were smoking their cigarettes and they smoking ours."

Another British sentry reported looking out toward the German lines, the enemy trenches were "all alight." "English soldiers! English soldiers!" challenged the German voices. "Happy Christmas! Where are your Christmas trees? No shoot tonight! Sing tonight!"

But the singing and the truce did not last. After a silent night and day—in many sectors much more than that—the war went on. Like a dream, when it was over men wondered at it, then went on with the grim business at hand. Under the rigid discipline of wartime command authority, that business was killing.

It was not that the troops in the trenches, condemned to costly stalemate, wanted to fight on, but that their governments did.

As an English major at the front lines in 1914 recalled, "I came to the conclusion that I have held very firmly ever since, that if we had been left to ourselves there would never have been another shot fired. We were on the most friendly terms, and it was only the fact that we were being controlled by others that made it necessary for us to start trying to shoot one another again."

As Playwright Bernard Shaw wrote "It is all hallucination, this war spirit; we all talk nonsense. German papers, French papers, English papers write the same article word for word (except the names), tell the same lies, believe the same impossible stories."

The event appears in retrospect somehow unreal, incredible in its intensity and extent, seemingly impossible to have happened without consequences for the outcome of the war.

Yet, Christmas 1914 evokes the stubborn humanity within us, and suggests an unrealized potential to burst its seams and rewrite a century. Although the unchanged reality of war is that the shots ordered by increasingly remote presences are absorbed by ordinary humans, Christmas 1914 reopened imaginations to the unsettling truth that at each end of the rifle, men were indeed the same.

—Stanley Weintraub

Adapted from *Silent Night: The Remarkable 1914 Christmas Truce*

What a powerful lesson of humanity: We are all one. What we really long for is peace more than power. May we remember these truths in all our interactions—global and personal. May we have the courage to act from our hearts instead of the outside forces of our individual or collective egos. May we surrender our thoughts of blame and attack, and may we join together with those who we have perceived as enemies to embrace the healing power of love.

Let's Dance

D. H. LAWRENCE ONCE WROTE THIS DEFINITION OF
ROMANCE: "AND WHAT'S ROMANCE? USUALLY, A NICE LITTLE
TALE WHERE YOU HAVE EVERYTHING AS YOU LIKE IT, WHERE
RAIN NEVER WETS YOUR JACKET AND GNATS NEVER BITE YOUR
NOSE AND IT'S ALWAYS DAISY-TIME."

I THINK MANY OF US HAVE HAD SIMILAR CONCEPTS ABOUT
ONE OF LIFE'S MOST BEAUTIFUL EXPERIENCES. THE ROMANCE
I EXPERIENCED WITH MY LATE WIFE CAUSED ME TO SEE A
DEEPER MEANING.
—*REV. STAN HOWSE*

DURING THE FINAL STAGES of terminal illness, various bodily functions cease to function properly. So it was with my beloved Rosemary. During her first round of chemotherapy, and the weeks immediately preceding her death almost two years later, this beautiful life partner of mine began to experience incontinence.

For Rosemary, who always dressed herself elegantly with tedious attention to details, this loss of control was especially devastating and humiliating. At times, it seemed the most horrifying aspect of her journey with cancer.

To one who took such great pride in her personal appearance and held so tightly to her independence and dignity by insisting she could take care of herself (she was my favorite "feminist"), being unable to control her bladder or bowels was no less than a disaster. It was almost more than either of us could bear. As proud as I was when I beheld her striking appearance in her Sunday best, my heart sank at the sounds in the night of her cries for help.

I would jump from our bed and race to the other side, hastily trying to help her in her physically weakened state to make it to the toilet. She was a petite brunette, and her weight loss due to her ill-ness made it easy to carry her small frame. I had learned from her oncologist a gentle way to lift her. First, I would bend over her body placing one hand on either side as she clasped her hands behind my neck and held as tightly as she could. Then I would raise my own body simultaneously hoisting her to the side of the bed, from where I could encircle her waist in my arms and half-carry, half-walk her to the commode.

Depending on the degree of sedation she was under at the time, or the intake of chemicals she had been given to fight the cancer, it seemed at times like I was practically dragging her body. After a few times, practice began to make it easier, and we could syn-chronize our movements and work more smoothly through the process.

Although in time and with repetition the procedure required less effort physically, facility did not ease the pain of her embar-rassment and emotional distress. It must have come as an intu-itive insight, a "heart thought," when one day as we were about to go through this difficult and awkward process once more, the idea came to me, "Let's dance!"

As I whispered these words, I watched her lift her head, look into my eyes, and give me a halting half-smile. Then she nodded, and we imagined ourselves on a ballroom floor as we waltzed to the nearby bathroom. From then on, the all-too-frequent attacks of helplessness became signals for a romantic interlude in a sea of despair. A time to lift our hearts together to a higher view of life, to laugh even, and to remember the love we shared and the faith we had in each other and in the ultimate goodness of life and God and the Universe.

As I recall those romantic moments, when every rational thought declared we ought not—we laughed and loved and held each other in pure delight. We always insisted on having fun, and together we learned to dance the dance of life as one.

We never stopped believing in the power of our love, and even though she is gone from my sight, it's as if she is right here beside me, cheering me on, reminding me that life goes on forever. So will the memory of our love, as we dance together in my heart for eternity.

—Rev. Stan Howse

In every instance—no matter how sad or helpless we feel—love can transform a moment of darkness into a moment of light.

bibliography

Bach, Richard.*Illusions: The Adventures of a Reluctant Messiah.* New York: Dell, 1977.

Beamer, Lisa.*Let's Roll: Ordinary People, Extraordinary Courage.* Wheaton, Illinois: Tyndale, 2002.

Beck, Charlotte Joko. *Everyday Zen.* San Francisco: HarperSanFrancisco, 1989.

Black, JoAnne et al. *Gandhi, the Man.* San Francisco: Glide, 1973.

Chödrön, Pema. *Start Where You Are: A Guide to Compassionate Living.* Boston: Shambhala, 1994.

A Course in Miracles. Tiburon, CA: Foundation for Inner Peace, 1985.

Fielding, Helen. *Bridget Jones's Diary.* New York: Penguin Books, 1996.

Fox, Michael J. *Lucky Man: A Memoir.* New York: Hyperion, 2002.

Holy Bible. Nashville, TN: Thomas Nelson, 1984.

Katie, Byron. *Loving What Is: Four Questions That Can Change Your Life.* New York: Harmony Books, 2002.

King, Martin Luther, Jr. *Strength to Love.* Philadelphia: Fortress Press, 1981.

Luskin, Fred. *Forgive for Good: A Proven Prescription for Health and Happiness.* San Francisco: HarperSanFrancisco, 2002.

Ogilvy, James. *Living Without a Goal: Finding the Freedom to Live a Creative and Innovative Life.* New York: Currency Doubleday, 1995.

Roy, Denise. *My Monastery Is a Minivan: Where the Daily Is Divine and the Routine Becomes Prayer.* Chicago: Loyola Press, 2001. "

Ryan, M. J. *Attitudes of Gratitude: How to Give and Receive Joy Every Day of Your Life.* Berkeley, CA: Conari Press, 1999.

Schwager, Jack D. *The New Market Wizards: Conversations with America's Top Traders.* New York: HarperBusiness, 1992.

Sher, Barbara. *I Could Do Anything If I Only Knew What It Was: How to Discover What You Really Want and How to Get It.* New York: Delacorte, 1994.

Sun Tzu. *The Art of War.* Trans. by Samuel B. Griffith. London: Oxford University Press, 1963.

Weintraub, Stanley. *Silent Night: The Remarkable 1914 Christmas Truce.* New York: The Free Press, 2001.

Williamson, Marianne. *A Return to Love: Reflections on the Principles of* A Course in Miracles. New York: HarperCollins, 1992.

Zukov, Gary. *The Seat of the Soul.* New York: Simon & Schuster, 1989.

contributors

Jill Althouse-Wood is an artist, writer, wife, and mother (in the order these titles appeared in her life). She is the co-author of *The Ornament,* a Christmas novella. She lives in Reinholds, Pennsylvania, with her husband and two children.

John D. Ashworth is a freelance writer and minister living in Georgia. He is completing his first novel.

Chandra Moira Beal is a writer and bodyworker in Austin, Texas. To learn more, visit *www.beal-net.com/soma.*

Dianne De Mink works as a personal chef and writer in Hot Springs, Arkansas. She is currently working on a book about designing the diabetic diet.

Lain Chroust Ehmann is a freelance writer in northern California, where she lives with her family. She is at work on her first novel, a mystery. You can reach her at *lainemann@comcast.net.*

Barbara S. Greenstreet is a freelance writer and educator from western Washington state. She is a lifelong, active member of the United Church of Christ. Barbara writes frequently on parenting, child development, education, and family relationships, as well as essays on issues and experiences related to spirituality and faith.

Sarah Holcombe, a Mississippi resident, is a wife and mother of two sons. She works in the newsroom of the *Daily Leader,* a local newspaper.

Ann Hood is the author of several novels and works of nonfiction, including *In Search of Miracles*. She lives in Providence, Rhode Island.

Rev. Stan Howse is a Unity minister in Burbank, California. He is happily remarried to a beautiful and charming lady.

Gerald Jampolsky, M.D., is a psychiatrist, formerly on the faculty of the University of California Medical Center in San Francisco. He is the founder of the Center for Attitudinal Healing in Sausalito, California, and a fellow of the American Psychiatric Association. Jampolsky's writings have been largely inspired by *A Course in Miracles*. He currently lectures and writes with his wife, therapist Diane Cirincione, Ph.D.

Dr. Julie Johnson is the senior minister of the Unity Community Church of Brea: A Center for Positive Living in Brea, California. She is a life coach, counselor, Reiki Master, and seminar leader.

Marie Jones is a New Thought minister and widely published writer of inspirational essays, gift books, short stories, and magazine articles. She has produced a children's storybook video series for Gigglebug Farms Productions as well as several direct-to-video projects. She holds a master's degree in metaphysical studies.

Heide Kaminski lives in Michigan with her husband and three children. She writes for a bimonthly newspaper in Lenawee County and for a monthly spiritual newsletter. She had her first book published in 1982 in Germany.

Anika Logan is a pseudonym.

Steve D. McRee is Executive Director of Shepherd's Gate, a shelter providing services and housing for battered and homeless women and children in Livermore, California. His wife, Carla, is Associate Director.

Amy Moellering is a writer and mother of three children. She lives in northern California.

Edward Mason Morgan lives and works in Mountain View, California, as a writer and marketing consultant.

Carrie Morris is happily married and enjoys life with her husband and two sons in northern California.

Juliann Nardone is Creative Director at Designing Words (*www.designing-words.com*), a writing, editing, and graphic design firm in Ashland, Massachusetts. She continues to recommend *Women Who Run with the Wolves* to women searching for their true paths through life.

Grace Mina Navalta lives with her husband, Ernesto, and their two children, Garret and Arianna, in Pleasanton, California. She manages a literacy program at the local library. She writes fiction and nonfiction articles for local publications.

Prader-Willi Syndrome occurs in 1 out of every 1,500 births. It is not inherited and can cause mental retardation, physical and behavioral problems, and is characterized by a life-threatening, insatiable urge to eat. Donations can be made to the PWS National Foundation.

Gina Romsdahl lives in the Sierra Nevada mountains of California. Her hobbies involve paper, be it cutting out pretty pictures, making collages, or occasionally writing on it. Several of her animal stories appear in the "Listening to the Animals" series of Guideposts Books.

Denise Roy is a mother of four, a psychotherapist, a spiritual director, and the founder of FamilySpirit, an organization that nurtures spirituality in families. She is the author of *My Monastery Is a Minivan: 35 Stories from a Real Life,* and lives with her family in the San Francisco Bay Area. You can read more on her website, *www.FamilySpirit.com.*

M.J. Ryan is the author of *The Power of Patience* and *Attitudes of Gratitude.*

Sunee Shelby lives in northern California with her three daughters.

Michelle Steele is a pseudonym.

Shelley Wake is a freelance writer from the Hunter Valley, Australia. Prior to becoming a writer, Shelley was a scientist and businesswoman and holds degrees in science, business and commerce.

Stanley Weintraub is Evan Pugh Professor Emeritus of Arts and Humanities at the Pennsylvania State University and the author of numerous histories and biographies. He lives in Boalsburg, Pennsylvania.

Donna J. Werstler is a writer and a church volunteer. She and her husband Mike share their home with their cat, Buddy, since their three children have married and moved away.

Patrick Wolff is two-time U.S. Chess Champion and author of *The Complete Idiot's Guide to Chess.* He resides in northern Virginia with his wife, Diana.

JoAnn Reno Wray is a freelance writer and editor from Broken Arrow, Oklahoma. She has had more than 450 articles, poems, and stories published and is the publisher-editor of *Melody of the Heart Ezine (www.epistleworks.com/HeartMelody).* She often speaks to church and women's groups and teaches at writers' conferences. Contact her at *epistle1@epistleworks.com.*

permissions

to our readers

CONARI PRESS, an imprint of Red Wheel/Weiser, publishes books on topics ranging from spirituality, personal growth, and relationships to women's issues, parenting, and social issues. Our mission is to publish quality books that will make a difference in people's lives—how we feel about ourselves and how we relate to one another. We value integrity, compassion, and receptivity, both in the books we publish and in the way we do business.

Our readers are our most important resource, and we value your input, suggestions, and ideas about what you would like to see published. Please feel free to contact us, to request our latest book catalog, or to be added to our mailing list.

Conari Press
An imprint of Red Wheel/Weiser, LLC
P.O. Box 612
York Beach, ME 03910-0612
www.conari.com